Although the author has made every effort to ensure that the information in this book was correct at the time of print, the author does not assume and hereby disclaim any liability to any party for any loss, damage, or disruption caused by errors or omissions, whether such errors or omissions result from negligence, accident, or any other cause.

© 2024 Taryn Dryfhout. All Rights Reserved.
www.TarynDryfhout.com

No part of this book may be reproduced or transmitted in any form or by any means, electronic or mechanical, including photocopying or recording, or by any information storage and retrieval system, without permission in writing from the publisher.

All photos and/or copyrighted material appearing in this book remains the work of its owners. Every effort has been made to give credit. No infringement is intended in this work. The title of this work, "You've Been Gilmored!: The Companion", as well as most of the chapter titles are phrases from *Gilmore Girls* and are not owned by the author. This book is not official, authorised by, or affiliated with The CW, Warner Brothers, Dorothy Parker Drank Here Productions or their representatives.

The Unofficial

You've Been Gilmored

Workbook

Taryn Dryfhout

Table of Contents

Introduction...7

I Smell Snow:
The Episodes..9

I Enjoy Watching People Watch Certain Parts of Certain Movies:
The Movies...19

So It's a Show? It's a Lifestyle. It's a Religion:
The Television Shows...39

I Live in Two Worlds. One is a World of Books:
The Books..49

Eternal Damnation is What I'm Risking for My Rock 'n' Roll:
The Music..67

It Takes Years of Training to Eat the Way We Do:
Eating Like a Gilmore..87

In Omnia Paratus:
The Bucket List..91

What She Tackles, She Conquers:
How to Study Like a Gilmore..101

Introduction

I said in my first book *You've Been Gilmored,* that what I wanted, more than anything, was to get my hands on a thoroughly comprehensive encyclopedia of all things *Gilmore Girls*. This need was met when I wrote *You've Been Gilmored,* but I realized after its publication, that a writable book where fans could record their Gilmore experiences, was missing. If *You've Been Gilmored* is a handbook for living a life that is thoroughly steeped in *Gilmore Girls,* then this book is where you can record it all.

If you have read my book, *You've Been Gilmored!,* then you will be familiar with the lists contained in this book. Some of these lists can be found in the 'Quickfire' section in *You've Been Gilmored!,* but in this companion book, the lists are designed to be worked through, and checked off as they are achieved. This functions as a workbook of sorts, where you can cross off tasks as you achieve each one, and can write notes in the margins (like Jess would), or in the note sections provided.

This book contains comprehensive lists from the *You've Been Gilmored* encyclopedia of every movie, television show, song, book, and food that every Gilmore fan should experience. In addition, it contains Rory's Study List and the *Gilmore Girls* Bucket List, which honorary Gilmore's can work through to immerse themselves in the "Gilmoreverse".

It is my hope that this book will allow you to experience a little more 'Gilmore'.

Taryn

I Smell Snow

Episode Directory

Season One

- ☐ Pilot
- ☐ The Lorelais' First Day at Chilton
- ☐ Kill Me Now
- ☐ The Deer Hunters
- ☐ Cinnamon's Wake
- ☐ Rory's Birthday Parties
- ☐ Kiss and Tell
- ☐ Love and War and Snow
- ☐ Rory's Dance
- ☐ Forgiveness and Stuff
- ☐ Paris Is Burning
- ☐ Double Date
- ☐ Concert Interruptus
- ☐ That Damn Donna Reed
- ☐ Christopher Returns
- ☐ Star-Crossed Lovers and Other Strangers
- ☐ The Breakup, Part 2
- ☐ The Third Lorelai
- ☐ Emily in Wonderland
- ☐ P.S. I Lo...
- ☐ Love, Daisies and Troubadours

Notes

Season Two

- c "Sadie, Sadie"
- c "Hammers and Veils"
- c "Red Light on the Wedding Night"
- c "The Road Trip to Harvard"
- c "Nick & Nora/Sid & Nancy"
- c "Presenting Lorelai Gilmore"
- c "Like Mother, Like Daughter"
- c "The Ins and Outs of Inns"
- c "Run Away, Little Boy"
- c "The Bracebridge Dinner"
- c "Secrets and Loans"
- c "Richard in Stars Hollow"
- c "A-Tisket, A-Tasket"
- c "It Should've Been Lorelai"
- c "Lost and Found"
- c "There's the Rub"
- c "Dead Uncles and Vegetables"
- c "Back in the Saddle Again"
- c "Teach Me Tonight"
- c "Help Wanted"
- c "Lorelai's Graduation Day"
- c "I Can't Get Started"

Notes

Season Three

- c Those Lazy-Hazy-Crazy Days
- c Haunted Leg
- c Application Anxiety
- c One's Got Class and the Other One Dyes
- c Eight O'Clock at the Oasis
- c Take the Deviled Eggs...
- c They Shoot Gilmores, Don't They?
- c Let the Games Begin
- c A Deep-Fried Korean Thanksgiving
- c That'll Do, Pig
- c I Solemnly Swear
- c Lorelai Out of Water
- c Dear Emily and Richard
- c Swan Song
- c Face-Off
- c The Big One
- c A Tale of Poes and Fire
- c Happy Birthday, Baby
- c Keg! Max!
- c Say Goodnight, Gracie
- c Here Comes the Son
- c Those Are Strings, Pinocchio

Notes

Season Four

- c Ballrooms and Biscotti
- c The Lorelais' First Day at Yale
- c The Hobbit, the Sofa and Digger Stiles
- c Chicken or Beef?
- c The Fundamental Things Apply
- c An Affair to Remember
- c The Festival of Living Art
- c Die, Jerk
- c Ted Koppel's Big Night Out
- c The Nanny and the Professor
- c In the Clamor and the Clangor
- c A Family Matter
- c Nag Hammadi Is Where They Found the Gnostic Gospels
- c The Incredible Sinking Lorelais
- c Scene in a Mall
- c The Reigning Lorelai
- c Girls in Bikinis, Boys Doin' The Twist
- c Tick, Tick, Tick, Boom!
- c Afterboom
- c Luke Can See Her Face
- c Last Week Fights, This Week Tights
- c Raincoats and Recipes

Notes

Season Five

- c Say Goodbye to Daisy Miller
- c A Messenger, Nothing More
- c Written in the Stars
- c Tippecanoe and Taylor, Too
- c We Got Us a Pippi Virgin
- c Norman Mailer, I'm Pregnant!
- c You Jump, I Jump, Jack
- c The Party's Over
- c Emily Says Hello
- c But Not as Cute as Pushkin
- c Women of Questionable Morals
- c Come Home
- c Wedding Bell Blues
- c Say Something
- c Jews and Chinese Food
- c So...Good Talk
- c Pulp Friction
- c To Live and Let Diorama
- c But I'm a Gilmore!
- c How Many Kropogs to Cape Cod?
- c Blame Booze and Melville
- c A House Is Not a Home

Notes

Season Six

- ☐ New and Improved Lorelai
- ☐ Fight Face
- ☐ The UnGraduate
- ☐ Always a Godmother, Never a God
- ☐ We've Got Magic to Do
- ☐ Welcome to the Doll House
- ☐ Twenty-One is the Loneliest Number
- ☐ Let Me Hear Your Balalaikas Ringing Out
- ☐ The Prodigal Daughter Returns
- ☐ He's Slippin' 'Em Bread...Dig?
- ☐ The Perfect Dress
- ☐ Just Like Gwen and Gavin
- ☐ Friday Night's Alright for Fighting
- ☐ You've Been Gilmored
- ☐ A Vineyard Valentine
- ☐ Bridesmaids Revisited
- ☐ I'm OK, You're OK
- ☐ The Real Paul Anka
- ☐ I Get a Sidekick Out of You
- ☐ Super Cool Party People
- ☐ Driving Miss Gilmore
- ☐ Partings

Notes

Season Seven

- c The Long Morrow
- c That's What You Get, Folks, for Makin' Whoopee
- c Lorelai's First Cotillion
- c 'S Wonderful, 'S Marvelous
- c The Great Stink
- c Go, Bulldogs!
- c French Twist
- c Introducing Lorelai Planetarium
- c Knit, People, Knit!
- c Merry Fisticuffs
- c Santa's Secret Stuff
- c To Whom It May Concern
- c I'd Rather Be in Philadelphia
- c Farewell, My Pet
- c I Am Kayak, Hear Me Roar
- c Will You Be My Lorelai Gilmore?
- c Gilmore Girls Only
- c Hay Bale Maze
- c It's Just Like Riding a Bike
- c Lorelai? Lorelai?
- c Unto the Breach
- c Bon Voyage

Notes

A Year in the Life

- c Winter
- c Spring
- c Summer
- c Fall

Notes

_____

_____

_____

_____

_____

_____

I Enjoy Watching people watch certain parts of certain movies

Movies

- ☐ 2 Fast 2 Furious (2003)
- ☐ 2001: A Space Odyssey (1968)
- ☐ 8 Mile (2002)
- ☐ 9½ Weeks (1986)
- ☐ A Beautiful Mind (2001)
- ☐ A Brief History of Time (1991)
- ☐ A History of Violence (2005)
- ☐ A Nightmare on Elm Street (1984)
- ☐ A Room with a View (1985)
- ☐ A Star Is Born (1976)
- ☐ A Streetcar Named Desire (1951)
- ☐ A Woman Under the Influence (1974)
- ☐ Accepted (2006)
- ☐ Ace Ventura: Pet Detective (1994)
- ☐ Al Capone (1959)
- ☐ Alice Doesn't Live Here Anymore (1974)
- ☐ Alice in Wonderland (1951)
- ☐ Alive (1993)
- ☐ All About Eve (1950)
- ☐ All the President's Men (1976)
- ☐ Almost Famous (2000)
- ☐ American Gigolo (1980)
- ☐ American Splendor (2003)
- ☐ An Affair to Remember (1957)
- ☐ An American in Paris (1951)
- ☐ An Inconvenient Truth (2006)
- ☐ An Officer and a Gentleman (1982)
- ☐ An Unmarried Woman (1978)
- ☐ Animal House (1978)
- ☐ Annie (1982)
- ☐ Annie Hall (1977)
- ☐ Anything Goes (1936)

- ☐ Anywhere But Here (1999)
- ☐ Apocalypse Now (1979)
- ☐ Arctic Flight (1952)
- ☐ Armageddon (1998)
- ☐ Arthur (1981)
- ☐ Attack of the 50 Foot Woman (1958)
- ☐ Austin Powers: The Spy Who Shagged Me (1999)
- ☐ Auto Focus (2002)
- ☐ Babe (1995)
- ☐ Babe: Pig in the City (1998)
- ☐ Babette: "Ah! I knew it! Simba, you've been dethroned."
- ☐ Baby Doll (1956)
- ☐ Back to the Future (1985)
- ☐ Bambi (1942)
- ☐ Barbarella (1968)
- ☐ Basic Instinct (1992)
- ☐ Batman v Superman: Dawn of Justice (2016)
- ☐ Beach Blanket Bingo (1965)
- ☐ Beaches (1988)
- ☐ Beethoven (1992)
- ☐ Being There (1979)
- ☐ Ben-Hur (1959)
- ☐ Bend It Like Beckham (2002)
- ☐ Benji (1974)
- ☐ Better Off Dead... (1985)
- ☐ Beverly Hills Cop (1984)
- ☐ Blades of Glory (2007)
- ☐ Blow (2001)
- ☐ Blue Crush (2002)
- ☐ Blue Velvet (1986)
- ☐ Bob & Carol & Ted & Alice (1969)

- ☐ Bonnie and Clyde (1967)
- ☐ Boogie Nights (1997)
- ☐ Boxing Helena (1993)
- ☐ Brazil (1985)
- ☐ Breakfast at Tiffany's (1961)
- ☐ Breakin' 2: Electric Boogaloo (1984)
- ☐ Breaking Away (1979)
- ☐ Bride of Chucky (1998)
- ☐ Bridget Jones's Diary (2001)
- ☐ Brigadoon (1954)
- ☐ Bright Eyes (1934)
- ☐ Bring Me the Head of Alfredo Garcia (1974)
- ☐ Bringing Up Baby (1938)
- ☐ Broadcast News (1987)
- ☐ Broadway Danny Rose (1984)
- ☐ Brokeback Mountain (2005)
- ☐ Bugsy (1991)
- ☐ Bugsy Malone (1976)
- ☐ Bull Durham (1988)
- ☐ Bullets Over Broadway (1994)
- ☐ Bullitt (1968)
- ☐ Butch Cassidy and the Sundance Kid (1969)
- ☐ Butterfield 8 (1960)
- ☐ Bye Bye Birdie (1963)
- ☐ Cabaret (1972)
- ☐ Cabin Boy (1994)
- ☐ Caged Heat (1974)
- ☐ Camelot (1967)
- ☐ Captain Corelli's Mandolin (2001)
- ☐ Carrie (1976)
- ☐ Casablanca (1942)
- ☐ Cats & Dogs (2001)

- [ ] Charlie's Angels: Full Throttle (2003)
- [ ] Chinatown (1974)
- [ ] Chitty Chitty Bang Bang (1968)
- [ ] Christine (1983)
- [ ] Christmas in July (1940)
- [ ] Cinderella (1950)
- [ ] Citizen Kane (1941)
- [ ] Cocktail (1988)
- [ ] Cocoon (1985)
- [ ] Coming Home (1978)
- [ ] Cool Hand Luke (1967)
- [ ] Cool as Ice (1991)
- [ ] Coyote Ugly (2000)
- [ ] Crimes and Misdemeanors (1989)
- [ ] Crouching Tiger, Hidden Dragon (2000)
- [ ] Cujo (1983)
- [ ] Damn Yankees! (1958)
- [ ] Dances with Wolves (1990)
- [ ] Dangerous Liaisons (1988)
- [ ] Das Boot (1981)
- [ ] David Blaine: Above the Below (2003)
- [ ] David and Lisa (1962)
- [ ] Dawn of the Dead (1978)
- [ ] Dead Calm (1989)
- [ ] Desperately Seeking Susan (1985)
- [ ] Destry Rides Again (1939)
- [ ] Deuce Bigalow: Male Gigolo (1999)
- [ ] Dig! (2004)
- [ ] Diner (1982)
- [ ] Dirty Dancing (1987)
- [ ] Divine Secrets of the Ya-Ya Sisterhood (2002)
- [ ] Doctor Dolittle (1967)
- [ ] Dog Day Afternoon (1975)

- ☐ Dogtown and Z-Boys (2001)
- ☐ Donnie Darko (2001)
- ☐ Dorf on Golf (1987)
- ☐ Double Indemnity (1944)
- ☐ Driving Miss Daisy (1989)
- ☐ Duck Soup (1933)
- ☐ Dumbo (1941)
- ☐ E.T. the Extra-Terrestrial (1982)
- ☐ Easter Parade (1948)
- ☐ Eastern Promises (2007)
- ☐ Easy Rider (1969)
- ☐ Eat Pray Love (2010)
- ☐ Ed Wood (1994)
- ☐ Edward Scissorhands (1990)
- ☐ Elizabeth (1998)
- ☐ Encino Man (1992)
- ☐ Endless Love (1981)
- ☐ Eraserhead (1977)
- ☐ Erin Brockovich (2000)
- ☐ Eternal Sunshine of the Spotless Mind (2004)
- ☐ Everest (1998)
- ☐ Face/Off (1997)
- ☐ Fahrenheit 9/11 (2004)
- ☐ Fame (1980)
- ☐ Farewell My Concubine (1993)
- ☐ Fast Times at Ridgemont High (1982)
- ☐ Fatal Attraction (1987)
- ☐ Fatso (1980)
- ☐ Ferris Bueller's Day Off (1986)
- ☐ Festival Express (2003)
- ☐ Fiddler on the Roof (1971)
- ☐ Field of Dreams (1989)

- [ ] Final Destination (2000)
- [ ] Final Destination 2 (2003)
- [ ] Final Destination 3 (2006)
- [ ] Firestarter (1984)
- [ ] Flashdance (1983)
- [ ] Fletch (1985)
- [ ] Footloose (1984)
- [ ] For Keeps? (1988)
- [ ] Frankenstein (1931)
- [ ] Freaky Friday (1976)
- [ ] Friday the 13th (1980)
- [ ] Fried Green Tomatoes (1991)
- [ ] From Here to Eternity (1953)
- [ ] From Justin to Kelly (2003)
- [ ] Full Metal Jacket (1987)
- [ ] Funny Face (1957)
- [ ] Funny Girl (1968)
- [ ] G.I. Jane (1997)
- [ ] Galaga (1981)
- [ ] Gangs of New York (2002)
- [ ] Gaslight (1944)
- [ ] Get Shorty (1995)
- [ ] Ghost (1990)
- [ ] Ghostbusters (1984)
- [ ] Giant (1956)
- [ ] Gidget (1959)
- [ ] Gigi (1958)
- [ ] Girl, Interrupted (1999)
- [ ] Girls Gone Wild on Campus 2 (2003)
- [ ] Give 'em Hell, Harry! (1975)
- [ ] Glitter
- [ ] Gone Girl (2014)
- [ ] Gone with the Wind (1939)

- ☐ Good Morning, Vietnam (1987)
- ☐ Goodfellas (1990)
- ☐ Grease (1978)
- ☐ Grey Gardens (1975)
- ☐ Gunga Din (1939)
- ☐ Guys and Dolls (1955)
- ☐ Halloween (1978)
- ☐ Happy Gilmore (1996)
- ☐ Hardbodies (1984)
- ☐ Harold and Maude (1971)
- ☐ Harry Potter and the Sorcerer's Stone (2001)
- ☐ Harvey (1950)
- ☐ Heathers (1988)
- ☐ Hello, Dolly! (1969)
- ☐ High Fidelity (2000)
- ☐ High Noon (1952)
- ☐ His Girl Friday (1940)
- ☐ Hitch (2005)
- ☐ Hoosiers (1986)
- ☐ Hotel Rwanda (2004)
- ☐ House of Flying Daggers (2004)
- ☐ House on Haunted Hill (1959)
- ☐ How the Grinch Stole Christmas! (1966)
- ☐ Hudson Hawk (1991)
- ☐ I Am a Camera (1955)
- ☐ Ice Castles (1978)
- ☐ Inside Llewyn Davis (2013)
- ☐ Inside Out (2015)
- ☐ Invasion of the Body Snatchers (1956)
- ☐ Invasion of the Body Snatchers (1978)
- ☐ Ishtar (1987)
- ☐ It Happened One Night (1934)

- [ ] It's a Wonderful Life (1946)
- [ ] Jack Frost (1998)
- [ ] Jackie Brown (1997)
- [ ] Jailhouse Rock (1957)
- [ ] Jarhead (2005)
- [ ] Jerry Maguire (1996)
- [ ] Jesus Christ Superstar (1973)
- [ ] Joe Versus the Volcano (1990)
- [ ] Julia (1977)
- [ ] Just Shoot Me! (1997)
- [ ] Kill Bill: Vol. 1 (2003)
- [ ] Killer Shark (1950)
- [ ] King Kong (1976)
- [ ] La Dolce Vita (1960)
- [ ] Lady and the Tramp (1955)
- [ ] Lassie (1954)
- [ ] Last Tango in Paris (1972)
- [ ] Legally Blonde (2001)
- [ ] Les Misérables (2012)
- [ ] Less Than Zero (1987)
- [ ] Life of Brian (1979)
- [ ] Life with Judy Garland: Me and My Shadows (2001)
- [ ] Like Father Like Son (1987)
- [ ] Little Man Tate (1991)
- [ ] Live and Let Die (1973)
- [ ] Looney, Looney, Looney Bugs Bunny Movie (1981)
- [ ] Lord Jim (1965)
- [ ] Lord of the Rings: The Return of the King (2003)
- [ ] Love Story (1970)
- [ ] Mad Hot Ballroom (2005)

- ☐ Mad Max Beyond Thunderdome (1985)
- ☐ Magnolia (1999)
- ☐ Mamma Mia! (2008)
- ☐ Marathon Man (1976)
- ☐ March of the Penguins (2005)
- ☐ Mary Poppins (1964)
- ☐ Mask (1985)
- ☐ Master and Commander: The Far Side of the World (2003)
- ☐ Mens vi venter på Godot (1965)
- ☐ Midnight Express (1978)
- ☐ Mildred Pierce (1945)
- ☐ Million Dollar Baby (1941)
- ☐ Misery (1990)
- ☐ Moment by Moment (1978)
- ☐ Mommie Dearest (1981)
- ☐ Monster (2003)
- ☐ Monty Python and the Holy Grail (1975)
- ☐ Moulin Rouge! (2001)
- ☐ Mr. & Mrs. Bridge (1990)
- ☐ Mr. Baseball (1992)
- ☐ My Fair Lady (1964)
- ☐ My Left Foot (1989)
- ☐ My Man Godfrey (1936)
- ☐ Mystic Pizza (1988)
- ☐ Nanny McPhee (2005)
- ☐ Nanook of the North (1922)
- ☐ Napoleon Dynamite (2004)
- ☐ National Treasure (2004)
- ☐ National Velvet (1944)
- ☐ Nell (1994)
- ☐ Network (1976)

- [ ] Norma Rae (1979)
- [ ] Not Without My Daughter (1991)
- [ ] Ocean's Eleven (2001)
- [ ] Oklahoma! (1955)
- [ ] Old Yeller (1957)
- [ ] Oliver Twist (1948)
- [ ] On the Town (1949)
- [ ] On the Waterfront (1954)
- [ ] Open Water (2003)
- [ ] Out of Africa (1985)
- [ ] Oxford Blues (1984)
- [ ] Panic Room (2002)
- [ ] Paper Moon (1973)
- [ ] Paris Is Burning (1990)
- [ ] Patton (1970)
- [ ] Peyton Place (1957)
- [ ] Pippi Långstrump (1969)
- [ ] Pleasantville (1998)
- [ ] Pretty in Pink (1986)
- [ ] Prizzi's Honor (1985)
- [ ] Psycho (1960)
- [ ] Pulp Fiction (1994)
- [ ] Purple Rain (1984)
- [ ] Queen of Outer Space (1958)
- [ ] Raging Bull (1980)
- [ ] Rain Man (1988)
- [ ] Rebecca of Sunnybrook Farm (1938)
- [ ] Rent (2005)
- [ ] Reservoir Dogs (1992)
- [ ] Reversal of Fortune (1990)
- [ ] Riding the Bus with My Sister (2005)
- [ ] Risky Business (1983)

- ☐ Robert Benchley and the Knights of the Algonquin (1998)
- ☐ RoboCop (1987)
- ☐ Rock of Ages (2012)
- ☐ Rocky (1976)
- ☐ Rocky III (1982)
- ☐ Roman Holiday (1953)
- ☐ Romeo + Juliet (1996)
- ☐ Rosemary's Baby (1968)
- ☐ Rudolph the Red-Nosed Reindeer (1964)
- ☐ Rush Hour (1998)
- ☐ Sabrina (1954)
- ☐ Saturday Night Fever (1977)
- ☐ Saving Private Ryan (1998)
- ☐ Saw II (2005)
- ☐ Say Anything... (1989)
- ☐ Scarface (1983)
- ☐ Scenes from a Mall (1991)
- ☐ Schindler's List (1993)
- ☐ Secrets & Lies (1996)
- ☐ Seven Brides for Seven Brothers (1954)
- ☐ Seven Samurai (1954)
- ☐ Shaft (1971)
- ☐ Shakespeare in Love (1998)
- ☐ Shall We Dance (1937)
- ☐ Shallow Hal (2001)
- ☐ Shane (1953)
- ☐ Shanghai Surprise (1986)
- ☐ Shields and Yarnell (1977)
- ☐ Shoah (1985)
- ☐ Showgirls (1995)
- ☐ Sid and Nancy (1986)

- ☐ Silent Movie (1976)
- ☐ Silkwood (1983)
- ☐ Singin' in the Rain (1952)
- ☐ Sister Act (1992)
- ☐ Six Candles (1984)
- ☐ Sleeping Beauty (1959)
- ☐ Sleepless in Seattle (1993)
- ☐ Snakes on a Plane (2006)
- ☐ Snow Dogs (2002)
- ☐ Snow White and the Seven Dwarfs (1937)
- ☐ Solaris (2002)
- ☐ Some Kind of Wonderful (1987)
- ☐ Song of the South (1946)
- ☐ Sophie's Choice (1982)
- ☐ South Pacific (1958)
- ☐ Speed (1994)
- ☐ St. Elmo's Fire (1985)
- ☐ Stalag 17 (1953)
- ☐ Star Trek: The Motion Picture (1979)
- ☐ Star Wars: Episode III - Revenge of the Sith (2005)
- ☐ Star Wars: Episode IV - A New Hope (1977)
- ☐ Star Wars: Episode V - The Empire Strikes Back (1980)
- ☐ Stop Making Sense (1984)
- ☐ Stuart Little (1999)
- ☐ Sudden Danger (1955)
- ☐ Summertime (1955)
- ☐ Sunset Boulevard (1950)
- ☐ Superman (1941)
- ☐ Suspense (1946)
- ☐ Sweet November (2001)
- ☐ Swept Away (2002)

- ☐ Swing Time (1936)
- ☐ Syriana (2005)
- ☐ Taxi Driver (1976)
- ☐ Tears and Laughter: The Joan and Melissa Rivers Story (1994)
- ☐ Terms of Endearment (1983)
- ☐ The 2000 Year Old Man (1975)
- ☐ The 40 Year Old Virgin (2005)
- ☐ The Adventures of Priscilla, Queen of the Desert (1994)
- ☐ The Amityville Horror (1979)
- ☐ The Arrival of a Train (1896)
- ☐ The Bad Seed (1956)
- ☐ The Banger Sisters (2002)
- ☐ The Blue Lagoon (1980)
- ☐ The Born Losers (1967)
- ☐ The Bourne Supremacy (2004)
- ☐ The Boy in the Plastic Bubble (1976)
- ☐ The Breakfast Club (1985)
- ☐ The Bridge on the River Kwai (1957)
- ☐ The Bridges of Madison County (1995)
- ☐ The Brown Bunny (2003)
- ☐ The Champ (1979)
- ☐ The Court Jester (1955)
- ☐ The Crucible (1996)
- ☐ The Deer Hunter (1978)
- ☐ The Exorcist (1973)
- ☐ The Fast and the Furious (2001)
- ☐ The Fast and the Furious: Tokyo Drift (2006)
- ☐ The Fly (1958)
- ☐ The Ghost and Mrs. Muir (1947)
- ☐ The Glass Menagerie (1950)

- ☐ The Glenn Miller Story (1954)
- ☐ The Godfather (1972)
- ☐ The Godfather: Part II (1974)
- ☐ The Godfather: Part III (1990)
- ☐ The Goofy Gophers (1947)
- ☐ The Goonies (1985)
- ☐ The Graduate (1967)
- ☐ The Grapes of Wrath (1940)
- ☐ The Great Santini (1979)
- ☐ The Great White Hope (1970)
- ☐ The Hunchback of Notre Dame (1996)
- ☐ The Hurt Locker (2008)
- ☐ The In-Laws (1979)
- ☐ The Incredible Shrinking Man (1957)
- ☐ The Jerk (1979)
- ☐ The Joy Luck Club (1993)
- ☐ The Jungle Book (2016)
- ☐ The Karate Kid (1984)
- ☐ The Lady Is Willing (1942)
- ☐ The Lake House (2006)
- ☐ The Last of the Mohicans (1992)
- ☐ The Legend of Bagger Vance (2000)
- ☐ The Lion King (1994)
- ☐ The Lord of the Rings: The Fellowship of the Ring (2001)
- ☐ The Lord of the Rings: The Two Towers (2002)
- ☐ The Lords of Flatbush (1974)
- ☐ The Lost Weekend (1945)
- ☐ The Lottery (1969)
- ☐ The Machinist (2004)
- ☐ The Magnificent Ambersons (1942)
- ☐ The Mambo Kings (1992)
- ☐ The Man Who Knew Too Much (1956)

- ☐ The Man in the Gray Flannel Suit (1956)
- ☐ The Manchurian Candidate (1962)
- ☐ The Matrix (1999)
- ☐ The Matrix Reloaded (2003)
- ☐ The Meaning of Life (1983)
- ☐ The Miracle Worker (1962)
- ☐ The Money Pit (1986)
- ☐ The Mothman Prophecies (2002)
- ☐ The Muse (1999)
- ☐ The Music Man (1962)
- ☐ The Naughty Nineties (1945)
- ☐ The Odd Couple (1968)
- ☐ The Omen (1976)
- ☐ The Outsiders (1983)
- ☐ The Parent Trap (1961)
- ☐ The Passion of the Christ (2004)
- ☐ The Pee Wee Herman Show (1981)
- ☐ The Perfect Storm (2000)
- ☐ The Philadelphia Story (1940)
- ☐ The Poseidon Adventure (1972)
- ☐ The Postman (1997)
- ☐ The Pursuit of Happyness (2006)
- ☐ The River Wild (1994)
- ☐ The Rocky Horror Picture Show (1975)
- ☐ The Shawshank Redemption (1994)
- ☐ The Shining (1980)
- ☐ The Silence of the Lambs (1991)
- ☐ The Singing Detective (1986)
- ☐ The Sixth Sense (1999)
- ☐ The Sound of Music (1965)
- ☐ The Stepford Wives (1975)
- ☐ The Sting (1973)

- ☐ The Thin Man (1934)
- ☐ The Thomas Crown Affair (1968)
- ☐ The Treasure of the Sierra Madre (1948)
- ☐ The Turning Point (1977)
- ☐ The Unbearable Lightness of Being (1988)
- ☐ The Way We Were (1973)
- ☐ The Witches of Eastwick (1987)
- ☐ The Wizard of Oz (1939)
- ☐ The Yearling (1946)
- ☐ Thelma & Louise (1991)
- ☐ Them! (1954)
- ☐ There Will Be Blood (2007)
- ☐ There's Something About Mary (1998)
- ☐ They Shoot Horses, Don't They? (1969)
- ☐ This Is Spinal Tap (1984)
- ☐ Three Days of the Condor (1975)
- ☐ Titanic (1997)
- ☐ To Kill a Mockingbird (1962)
- ☐ Tommy (1975)
- ☐ Top Gun (1986)
- ☐ Touch of Evil (1958)
- ☐ Trainspotting (1996)
- ☐ True Grit (1969)
- ☐ Tuesdays with Morrie (1999)
- ☐ Up (2009)
- ☐ Urban Cowboy (1980)
- ☐ Valentine (2001)
- ☐ Valley of the Dolls (1967)
- ☐ View from the Top (2003)
- ☐ Waiting for Guffman (1996)
- ☐ Wall Street (1987)
- ☐ Welcome to the Dollhouse (1995)
- ☐ West Side Story (1961)

- ☐ What Ever Happened to Baby Jane? (1962)
- ☐ Where Are Your Children? (1943)
- ☐ Who's Afraid of Virginia Woolf? (1966)
- ☐ Wild (2014)
- ☐ Willy Wonka & the Chocolate Factory (1971)
- ☐ Winnie the Pooh and the Honey Tree (1966)
- ☐ Wonder Woman: Who's Afraid of Diana Prince? (1967)
- ☐ Working Girl (1988)
- ☐ Xanadu (1980)
- ☐ Yellow Submarine (1968)
- ☐ Yentl (1983)
- ☐ You're a Good Man, Charlie Brown (1973)
- ☐ You've Got Mail (1998)
- ☐ Young Frankenstein (1974)
- ☐ Zoolander 2 (2016)

Notes

_____

_____

_____

_____

_____

_____

_____

It's a Lifestyle.
It's a Religion.

Television

- ☐ 21 Jump Street (1987)
- ☐ 24 (2001)
- ☐ 60 Minutes (1968)
- ☐ 7th Heaven (1996)
- ☐ ABC Afterschool Specials (1972)
- ☐ Absolutely Fabulous (1992)
- ☐ Alice (1976)
- ☐ All in the Family (1971)
- ☐ America's Next Top Model (2003)
- ☐ Angela's Ashes (1999)
- ☐ Animaniacs (1993)
- ☐ Antiques Roadshow (1997)
- ☐ Barefoot Contessa (2002)
- ☐ Baretta (1975)
- ☐ Batman (1966)
- ☐ BattleBots (2000)
- ☐ Battlestar Galactica (1978)
- ☐ Baywatch (1989)
- ☐ Behind the Music (1997)
- ☐ Benson (1979)
- ☐ Beverly Hills, 90210 (1990)
- ☐ Bewitched (1964)
- ☐ Blue Bloods (2010)
- ☐ Bosom Buddies (1980)
- ☐ Bozo (1960)
- ☐ Brian's Song (1971)
- ☐ Brideshead Revisited (1981)
- ☐ Buffy the Vampire Slayer (1997)
- ☐ CBS Evening News with Dan Rather (1981)
- ☐ CHiPs (1977)
- ☐ CSI: Miami (2002)
- ☐ Captain Kangaroo (1955)

- ☐ Charlie Rose (1991)
- ☐ Charlie's Angels (1976)
- ☐ Chico and the Man (1974)
- ☐ Columbo (1971)
- ☐ Cop Rock (1990)
- ☐ Cops (1989)
- ☐ Cribs (2000)
- ☐ Danger Mouse (1981)
- ☐ Daria (1997)
- ☐ Dark Shadows (1966)
- ☐ Dawson's Creek (1998)
- ☐ Days of Our Lives (1965)
- ☐ Deadwood (2004)
- ☐ Def Comedy Jam (1992)
- ☐ Desperate Housewives (2004)
- ☐ Diff'rent Strokes (1978)
- ☐ Doctor Who (1963)
- ☐ Doogie Howser, M.D. (1989)
- ☐ Dr. Phil (2002)
- ☐ Dynasty (1981)
- ☐ E! True Hollywood Story (1996)
- ☐ ER (1994)
- ☐ Electra Woman and Dyna Girl (1976)
- ☐ Everybody Loves Raymond (1996)
- ☐ Family Feud (1976)
- ☐ Family Matters (1989)
- ☐ Fantasy Island (1977)
- ☐ Fat Albert and the Cosby Kids (1972)
- ☐ Felicity (1998)
- ☐ Frontline (1983)
- ☐ Frosty the Snowman (1954)
- ☐ Full House (1987)

- ☐ Futurama (1999)
- ☐ Game of Thrones (2011)
- ☐ General Hospital (1963)
- ☐ Get Smart (1965)
- ☐ Gilligan's Island (1964)
- ☐ Girlfriends (2000)
- ☐ Gumby Adventures (1988)
- ☐ Halt and Catch Fire (2014)
- ☐ Happy Days (1974)
- ☐ Hart to Hart (1979)
- ☐ Hawaii Five-O (1968)
- ☐ Hee Haw (1969)
- ☐ Hee Haw Honeys (1978)
- ☐ Hogan's Heroes (1965)
- ☐ Holmes and Yo-Yo (1976)
- ☐ How the Grinch Stole Christmas! (1966)
- ☐ I Dream of Jeannie (1965)
- ☐ I Love Lucy (1951)
- ☐ Inside the Actors Studio (1994)
- ☐ Iron Chef (1993)
- ☐ Iron Chef America: The Series (2005)
- ☐ Jazz (2001)
- ☐ Jeopardy! (1984)
- ☐ Joanie Loves Chachi (1982)
- ☐ Johnny Bravo (1997)
- ☐ Joseph Campbell and the Power of Myth (1988)
- ☐ Kentucky vs. the University of Alabama, Freedom Hall - Louisville, Kentucky (January 21, 1998).
- ☐ Knots Landing: Moments of Truth (1981)
- ☐ Lassie (1954)
- ☐ Laugh-In (1967)
- ☐ Laverne & Shirley (1976)

- ☐ Law & Order (1990)
- ☐ Leave It to Beaver (1957)
- ☐ Les Revenants (2012)
- ☐ Lifestyles of the Rich and Famous (1984)
- ☐ Lillehammer 1994: XVII Olympic Winter Games (1994)
- ☐ Live! With Kelly and Michael (1988)
- ☐ Lost in Space (1965)
- ☐ M*A*S*H (1970)
- ☐ Magnum, P.I. (1980)
- ☐ Mahha GoGoGo (1967)
- ☐ Malcolm in the Middle (2000)
- ☐ Marcus Welby, M.D. (1969)
- ☐ Martha Stewart Living (1991)
- ☐ Matlock (1986)
- ☐ Meet the Press (1947)
- ☐ Mission: Impossible (1966)
- ☐ Mister Ed (1958)
- ☐ Monk (2002)
- ☐ Monty Python's Flying Circus (1969)
- ☐ Mutual of Omaha's Wild Kingdom (1963)
- ☐ My Little Pony Tales (1992)
- ☐ NFL Monday Night Football (1970)
- ☐ NYPD Blue (1993)
- ☐ Nancy Grace (2005)
- ☐ Nanny and the Professor (1970)
- ☐ Narcos (2015)
- ☐ Nigella Bites (2000)
- ☐ Outlander (2014)
- ☐ Oz (1997)
- ☐ Pee-wee's Playhouse (1986)
- ☐ Petticoat Junction (1963)

- [ ] Peyton Place (1964)
- [ ] Pink Lady (1980)
- [ ] Pippi Långstrump (1969)
- [ ] Please Don't Eat the Daisies (1965)
- [ ] Politically Incorrect (1993)
- [ ] Privileged: All About Friends and Family (2008)
- [ ] Project Runway (2004)
- [ ] Punk'd (2003)
- [ ] Puppet Playhouse (1947)
- [ ] Queer Eye for the Straight Guy (2003)
- [ ] Quincy M.E. (1976)
- [ ] Reno 911! (2003)
- [ ] Rhoda (1974)
- [ ] Ricki Lake (1992)
- [ ] Rock Star: INXS (2005)
- [ ] Sanford and Son (1972)
- [ ] Saturday Night Live (1975)
- [ ] Saved by the Bell (1989)
- [ ] Schindler's List (1993)
- [ ] Schoolhouse Rock! (1973)
- [ ] Scooby Doo, Where Are You! (1969)
- [ ] Seinfeld (1989)
- [ ] Sesame Street (1969)
- [ ] Sex and the City (1998)
- [ ] Shields and Yarnell (1977)
- [ ] Smurfs (1981)
- [ ] Soap (1977)
- [ ] Soul Train (1971)
- [ ] Soulcalibur III (2005)
- [ ] South Park (1997)
- [ ] SpongeBob SquarePants (1999)
- [ ] Star Search (1983)
- [ ] Star Trek (1966)

- ☐ Star Trek: The Next Generation (1987)
- ☐ Summerland (2004)
- ☐ Survivor (2000)
- ☐ Sábado Gigante (1962)
- ☐ Taxi (1978)
- ☐ Teenage Mutant Ninja Turtles (1987)
- ☐ Teletubbies (1997)
- ☐ That Girl (1966)
- ☐ The 67th Annual Academy Awards (1995)
- ☐ The 700 Club (1966)
- ☐ The 75th Annual Academy Awards (2003)
- ☐ The 78th Annual Academy Awards (2006)
- ☐ The Addams Family (1964)
- ☐ The Amazing Race (2001)
- ☐ The Andy Griffith Show (1960)
- ☐ The Apprentice (2004)
- ☐ The Brady Bunch (1969)
- ☐ The Brady Bunch Variety Hour (1976)
- ☐ The Comeback (2005)
- ☐ The Courtship of Eddie's Father (1969)
- ☐ The Daily Show (1996)
- ☐ The Dick Van Dyke Show (1961)
- ☐ The Donna Reed Show (1958)
- ☐ The Dukes of Hazzard (1979)
- ☐ The Flintstones (1960)
- ☐ The Greatest American Hero (1981)
- ☐ The Gumby Show (1956)
- ☐ The Honeymooners (1955)
- ☐ The Jetsons (1962)
- ☐ The Kids in the Hall (1988)
- ☐ The L Word (2004)
- ☐ The Late Show with David Letterman (1993)

- ☐ The Lawrence Welk Show (1951)
- ☐ The Life and Times of Grizzly Adams (1977)
- ☐ The Little Rascals (1955)
- ☐ The Lonely Island: Lazy Sunday (2005)
- ☐ The Love Boat (1977)
- ☐ The Monkees (1966)
- ☐ The Munsters (1964)
- ☐ The Muppet Show (1976)
- ☐ The Mysteries of Laura (2014)
- ☐ The O.C. (2003)
- ☐ The Odd Couple (1970)
- ☐ The Office (2001)
- ☐ The Oprah Winfrey Show (1986)
- ☐ The Patty Duke Show (1963)
- ☐ The Powerpuff Girls (1998)
- ☐ The Price Is Right (1972)
- ☐ The Real World (1992)
- ☐ The Simpsons (1989)
- ☐ The Six Million Dollar Man (1973)
- ☐ The Sonny and Cher Show (1976)
- ☐ The Sopranos (1999)
- ☐ The Tonight Show (1962)
- ☐ The Twilight Zone (1959)
- ☐ The View (1997)
- ☐ The Voice (2011)
- ☐ The Waltons (1971)
- ☐ The West Wing (1999)
- ☐ The Yogi Bear Show (1961)
- ☐ Thirtysomething (1987)
- ☐ This Is Your Life (1952)
- ☐ This Old House (1979)
- ☐ Toast of the Town: Episode #17.19 (1964)
- ☐ Today (1952)

- ☐ Top Chef (2006)
- ☐ Total Request Live (1998)
- ☐ Two Fat Ladies (1996)
- ☐ Two and a Half Men (2003)
- ☐ V.I.P. (1998)
- ☐ Wheel of Fortune (1983)
- ☐ Who's the Boss? (1984)
- ☐ Will & Grace (1998)
- ☐ Wonder Woman (1975)
- ☐ Xuxa (1993)

Notes

I Live in Two Worlds. One is a World of Books

Books

- ☐ 18 and Life on Skid Row by Sebastian Bach
- ☐ 1984 by George Orwell
- ☐ A Bolt from The Blue and Other Essays by Mary McCarthy
- ☐ A Christmas Carol by Charles Dickens
- ☐ A Clockwork Orange by Anthony Burgess
- ☐ A Confederacy of Dunces by John Kennedy Toole
- ☐ A Connecticut Yankee in King Arthur's Court by Mark Twain
- ☐ A Girl from Yamhill, Beverly Cleary; Like Water for Chocolate by Laura Esquivel
- ☐ A Heartbreaking Work of Staggering Genius by Dave Eggers
- ☐ A Mencken's Chrestomathy by H.L. Mencken
- ☐ A Monetary History of the United States by Milton Friedman
- ☐ A Moveable Feast by Ernest Hemingway
- ☐ A Room of One's Own by Virginia Woolf
- ☐ A Room with a View by E.M. Forster
- ☐ A Streetcar Named Desire by Tennessee Williams
- ☐ A Tale of Two Cities by Charles Dickens
- ☐ Absolute Rage by Robert K Tanenbaum
- ☐ Alice's Adventures in Wonderland by Lewis Carroll
- ☐ All the Pretty Horses by Cormac McCarthy
- ☐ American Steel by Richard Preston
- ☐ Angels in America by Tony Kushner
- ☐ Anna Karenina by Leo Tolstoy
- ☐ As I Lay Dying by William Faulkner
- ☐ Atonement by Ian McEwan
- ☐ Babe by Dick King- Smith

- ☐ Backlash: The Undeclared War Against American Women by Susan Faludi
- ☐ Bad Dirt by Annie Proulx
- ☐ Basic Writings of Nietzsche by Friedrich Nietzsche
- ☐ Beowulf by unknown
- ☐ Beyond Good and Evil by Friedrich Nietzsche
- ☐ Billy Budd and Other Tales, Herman Melville
- ☐ Blind Faith by Joe McGinniss
- ☐ Brave New World by Aldous Huxley
- ☐ Brigadoon by Alan Jay Lerner
- ☐ Brothers on Life by Matt Czuchry and Mike Czuchry
- ☐ But I'm a Gilmore by Taryn Dryfhout
- ☐ Call of the Wild by Jack London
- ☐ Candide by Voltaire
- ☐ Carrie by Stephen King
- ☐ Catch-22 by Joseph Heller
- ☐ Charles Darwin, On the Origin of Species
- ☐ Charlie and the Chocolate Factory by Roald Dahl
- ☐ Charlotte's Web by E.B. White
- ☐ Chronicles of Narnia by C.S. Lewis
- ☐ Chrysanthemum by Kevin Henkes
- ☐ Clifford the Big Red Dog by Norman Bridwell
- ☐ Cloud Atlas by David Mitchell
- ☐ Coffee at Luke's: An Unauthorized Gilmore Girls Gabfest by Leah Wilson
- ☐ Complete Novels by Dawn Powell
- ☐ Consider the Lobster by David Foster Wallace
- ☐ Contact by Carl Sagan
- ☐ Contemporary Political Fiction
- ☐ Cujo by Stephen King

- ☐ Cyrano de Bergerac by Edmond Rostand
- ☐ David and Lisa by Dr Theodore Issac Rubin M.D.
- ☐ David Copperfield by Charles Dickens
- ☐ Dead Souls by Nikolai Vasilevich Gogol
- ☐ Death of a Salesman by Arthur Miller
- ☐ Deenie by Judy Blume
- ☐ Delta of Venus by Anais Nin
- ☐ Demons by Fyodor Dostoevsky; translated by Richard Pevear and Larissa Volokhonsky
- ☐ Don Quixote by Miguel de Cervantes
- ☐ Downpour by Nick Holmes
- ☐ Dr. Dolittle by Hugh Lofting
- ☐ Driving Miss Daisy by Alfred Uhry
- ☐ Eat Like a Gilmore: Daily Cravings by Kristi Carlson
- ☐ Eat Like a Gilmore: The Unofficial Cookbook for Fans of Gilmore Girls by Kristi Carlson
- ☐ Eat Like a Gilmore: Seasons by Kristi Carlson
- ☐ Eat, Pray, Love by Elizabeth Gilbert
- ☐ Eleanor Roosevelt by Blanche Wiesen Cook
- ☐ Elements by Euclid
- ☐ Elmer Gantry by Sinclair Lewis
- ☐ Eloise by Kay Thompson
- ☐ Emily the Strange by Roger Reger
- ☐ Encyclopedia Brown: Boy Detective by Donald J. Sobol
- ☐ Essentials of Economics, 3rd ed., Bradley R. Schiller
- ☐ Ethan Frome by Edith Wharton
- ☐ Ethics by Spinoza
- ☐ Europe Through the Back Door, 2003 by Rick Steves

- ☐ Eva Luna by Isabel Allende
- ☐ Fast Talk & Faith: A 22-Day Devotional Inspired by Gilmore Girls
- ☐ Fear and Loathing in Las Vegas by Hunter S. Thompson
- ☐ Firewall by Lawrence E. Walsh
- ☐ First Folio by William Shakespeare
- ☐ Flavor of the Month by Olivia Goldsmith
- ☐ Fletch by Gregory McDonald
- ☐ Frankenstein by Mary Shelley
- ☐ Franny and Zooey by J.D. Salinger
- ☐ Freaky Friday by Mary Rodgers
- ☐ Frida by Hayden Herrera
- ☐ Gabfest by Leah Wilson
- ☐ Game of Thrones by George R.R. Martin
- ☐ Gender Trouble by Judith Butler
- ☐ Gidget by Frederick Kohner
- ☐ Gigi by Collette
- ☐ Gilmore Girls and the Politics of Identity: Essays on Family and Feminism in the Television Series by Ritch Calvin
- ☐ Gilmore Girls: A Cultural History by Lara C. Stache, Rachel Davidson
- ☐ Gilmore Girls: I Do, Don't I? (Book 3) by Catherine Clark
- ☐ Gilmore Girls: I Love You, You Idiot (Book 2) by Cathy East Dubowski
- ☐ Gilmore Girls: Like Mother, Like Daughter (Book 1) by Catherine Clark
- ☐ Gilmore Girls: The Other Side of Summer (Book 4) by Helen Pai
- ☐ Girl, Interrupted by Susanna Kaysen
- ☐ Glengarry Glen Ross by David Mamet
- ☐ Go Set a Watchman by Harper Lee

- ☐ Gone with the Wind by Margaret Mitchell
- ☐ Goodnight Moon by Margaret Wise Brown and Clement Hurd
- ☐ Grandma Told Me So: Lessons in Life and Love by Carla McCloskey
- ☐ Great Expectations by Charles Dickens
- ☐ Gulliver's Travels by Jonathon Swift
- ☐ Guys and Dolls by Jo Swerling and Abe Burrows
- ☐ Haiku, Volume 2: Spring by R.H. Blyth
- ☐ Haiti: State Against Nation: Origins and Legacy of Duvalierism by Michel-Rolph Trouillot
- ☐ Hamlet by William Shakespeare
- ☐ Harold and the Purple Crayon by Crockett Johnson
- ☐ Harry Potter & the Goblet of Fire by J.K. Rowling
- ☐ Harry Potter and the Sorcerer's Stone: Harry Potter - Book 1 by J. K. Rowling
- ☐ He's Just Not That Into You by Greg Behrendt and Liz Tuccillo
- ☐ Henry IV, Part 1 by William Shakespeare
- ☐ Henry IV, Part 2 by William Shakespeare
- ☐ Henry V by William Shakespeare
- ☐ Hidden Romantic Gems of the Restaurant World
- ☐ High Fidelity by Nick Hornsby
- ☐ History of the Peloponnesian War by Thucydides
- ☐ Hockey for Dummies by John Davidson
- ☐ Hoover's Handbook of American Business 1996 by Gary Hoover
- ☐ How the Grinch Stole Christmas by Dr. Seuss

- ☐ How we are Hungry by Dave Eggers
- ☐ Howl by Allen Ginsberg
- ☐ Huckleberry Finn by Mark Twain
- ☐ I Feel Bad About My Neck: And Other Thoughts on Being a Woman by Nora Ephron
- ☐ I'm With the Band by Pamela Des Barres
- ☐ In Cold Blood by Truman Capote
- ☐ In Conclusion, Don't Worry About It by Lauren Graham
- ☐ In Search of Lost Time by Marcel Proust
- ☐ In the Shadow of Young Girls in Flower by Marcel Proust
- ☐ Inferno by Dante
- ☐ Inherit the Wind by Jerome Lawrence and Robert E. Lee
- ☐ Into the Woods by Stephen Sondheim
- ☐ Iron Weed by William J. Kennedy
- ☐ It Takes a Village by Hilary Clinton
- ☐ Jaglon by Asher Fleming (fictional text)
- ☐ Jane Eyre by Charlotte Bronte
- ☐ Jane: One Woman's Harrowing Journey to God (fictional text)
- ☐ Julius Caesar by William Shakespeare
- ☐ King Richard III by William Shakespeare
- ☐ Lady Chatterley's Lover by D.H. Lawrence
- ☐ Laroose Wine by David Cobbold
- ☐ Leaves of Grass by Walt Whitman
- ☐ Less than Zero, Bret Easton Ellis
- ☐ Letters of Ayn Rand edited by Michael S. Berliner
- ☐ Letters to a Young Poet by Rainer Maria Rilke
- ☐ Lies and the Lying Liars Who Tell Them by Al Franken

- [ ] Life of Samuel Johnson by James Boswell
- [ ] Like Water for Chocolate by Laura Esquivel
- [ ] Little Dorrit by Charles Dickens
- [ ] Little House in the Big Woods by Laura Ingalls Wilder
- [ ] Little House on the Prairie by Laura Ingalls Wilder
- [ ] Lolita by Vladimir Nabokov
- [ ] Lord Jim by Joseph Conrad
- [ ] Lord of the Flies by William Golding
- [ ] Lord of The Rings: The Return of the King by J.R.R. Tolkien
- [ ] Love Story, Erich Segal
- [ ] Macbeth by William Shakespeare
- [ ] Madame Bovary by Gustave Flaubert
- [ ] Madeline by Ludwig Bemelmans
- [ ] Marathon Man by William Goldman
- [ ] Martha Stewart Living, Holidays: The Best of Martha Stewart Living
- [ ] Matisse the Master: A Life of Henri Matisse by Hilary Spurling
- [ ] Memoirs of a Dutiful Daughter by Simone de Beauvoir
- [ ] Memoirs of General W. T. Sherman by William Tecumseh Sherman
- [ ] Mencken's Chrestomathy by H.R. Mencken
- [ ] Mistress of Mellyn by Victoria Holt
- [ ] Moby Dick by Herman Melville
- [ ] Moliere: A Biography by Hobart Chatfield Taylor
- [ ] Mommie Dearest by Christina Crawford
- [ ] Monsieur Proust by Celeste Albaret
- [ ] Mrs. Dalloway by Virginia Woolf

- ☐ Mutiny on the Bounty by Charles Nordhoff and James Norman Hall
- ☐ My First Summer in the Sierra by John Muir
- ☐ My Lai 4: A Report on the Massacre and Its Aftermath by Seymour M. Hersh
- ☐ My Life as Author and Editor by H.L. Mencken
- ☐ My Struggle by Karl Ove Knausgaard
- ☐ Myra Waldo's Travel and Motoring Guide to Europe, 1978 by Myra Waldo
- ☐ Naked Lunch: The Restored Text, William S. Burroughs
- ☐ Nancy Drew 33: The Witch Tree Symbol by Carolyn Keene
- ☐ Nancy Drew Mysteries by Carolyn Keene
- ☐ Native Son by Richard Wright
- ☐ Nature's Metropolis: Chicago and the Great West by William Cronon
- ☐ Nickel and Dimed by Barbara Ehrenreich
- ☐ No Man is an Island by John Donne
- ☐ No Mistakes: A Workbook for Imperfect Artists by Keiko Agena
- ☐ Northanger Abbey by Jane Austen
- ☐ Notes of a Dirty Old Man by Charles Bukowski
- ☐ November of the Heart by LaVyrle Spencer
- ☐ Of Human Bondage by W Somerset Maugham
- ☐ Of Mice and Men by John Steinbeck
- ☐ Oliver Twist by Charles Dickens
- ☐ On the Contrary by Mary McCarthy
- ☐ On the Road by Jack Kerouac
- ☐ One Day in the Life of Ivan Denisovich by Aleksandr Solzhenitsyn
- ☐ One Hundred Years of Solitude by Gabriel Garcia Marquez
- ☐ Orations of American Orators

- ☐ Othello by William Shakespeare
- ☐ Out of Africa by Isaac Denison
- ☐ Outlander by Diana Gabaldon
- ☐ *Oxford English Dictionary*
- ☐ Personal History by Katharine Graham
- ☐ Peyton Place by Grace Metalious
- ☐ Pinocchio by Carlo Collodi
- ☐ Please Kill Me: The Uncensored Oral History of Punk by Legs McNeil and Gillian McCain
- ☐ *Plutarch's Lives, volume 1 or 2 by* John Dryden and Arthur Hugh Clough
- ☐ Poems by Alfred Lord Tennyson
- ☐ Points of View by W Somerset Maugham
- ☐ Pomeranian: An Owner's Guide to a Happy Healthy Pet by Happeth A. Jones
- ☐ Punk: The Definitive Record of a Revolution by Stephen Colegrave and Colin Sullivan
- ☐ Pushkin: A Biography by T.J. Binyon
- ☐ Quiller Bambo by Adam Hall
- ☐ R is for Ricochet by Sue Grafton
- ☐ Rapunzel by Brothers Grimm
- ☐ Rebecca of Sunnybrook Farm by Kate Douglas Wiggin
- ☐ Revolution from Within by Gloria Steinem
- ☐ Rita Hayworth and The Shawshank Redemption by Stephen King
- ☐ Robert's Rules of Order by Henry Robert
- ☐ Romeo and Juliet by William Shakespeare
- ☐ Rosemary's Baby by Ira Levin
- ☐ S is for Silence by Sue Grafton
- ☐ Sailing Alone Around the Room: New and Selected Poems by Billy Collins

- ☐ Savage Beauty: The Life of Edna St. Vincent Millay by Nancy Milford
- ☐ Saving the Queen by William F. Buckley Jr.
- ☐ Say Goodbye to Daisy Miller by Henry James
- ☐ Screwball Television: Critical Perspectives on Gilmore Girls by David Lavery and David Scott Diffrient
  Fast Talk & Faith: A 22-Day Devotional Inspired by Gilmore Girls by Mary Carver
- ☐ Secrets of the Flesh: A Life of Colette by Judith Thurman
- ☐ Selected Hotels of Europe
- ☐ Sexus by Henry Miller
- ☐ Sherlock Holmes by Arthur Conan Doyle
- ☐ Silly Lop by Biff Yeager
- ☐ Slaughter-House Five by Kurt Vonnegut
- ☐ Snow White and Rose Red by Grimm Brothers
- ☐ Snows of Kilimanjaro by Ernest Hemingway
- ☐ Smokey the Cat by Biff Yeager
- ☐ Social Origins of Dictatorship and Democracy by Barrington Moore Jr.
- ☐ Someday, Someday, Maybe by Lauren Graham
- ☐ Sophie's Choice by William Styron
- ☐ Stalin: A Biography by Robert Service
- ☐ Stepford Wives by Ira Levin
- ☐ Story of O by Pauline Reage
- ☐ Stuart Little by E. B. White
- ☐ Summer of Fear by T Jefferson Parker
- ☐ Swann's Way by Marcel Proust
- ☐ Taken Hostage: the Iran Hostage Crisis and America's First Encounter with Radical Islam by David Farber
- ☐ Talking as Fast As I Can by Lauren Graham
- ☐ Tender is the Night by F Scott Fitzgerald

- [ ] Terms of Endearment by Larry McMurtry
- [ ] Tevya the Dairyman and the Railroad Stories by Sholem Aleichem
- [ ] The Adventures of Huckleberry Finn by Mark Twain
- [ ] The Age of Innocence by Edith Wharton
- [ ] The Andy Warhol Diaries edited by Pat Hackett
- [ ] The Apocalyptics - Cancer and the Big Lie: How Environmental Politics Controls What We Know About Cancer by Edith Efron
- [ ] The Armies of the Night: History as a Novel, the Novel as History; The Executioner's Song by Norman Mailer
- [ ] The Art of Eating by MFK Fisher
- [ ] The Art of Fiction by Henry James
- [ ] The Art of War by Sun Tzu
- [ ] The Bell Jar by Sylvia Plath
- [ ] The Bhagavad Gita
- [ ] The Bible
- [ ] The Big Love by Sarah Dunn
- [ ] The Bright of Martydom (fictional text)
- [ ] The Brontes by Juliet Barker
- [ ] The Catcher in the Rye by J.D. Salinger
- [ ] The Children's Hour by Lillian Hellman
- [ ] The Collected Short Stories by Eudora Welty
- [ ] The Compact Oxford English Dictionary by Henry Watson Fowler
- [ ] The Complete Poems by Anne Sexton
- [ ] The Complete Works of William Shakespeare by William Shakespeare
- [ ] The Crimson Petal and the White by Michel Faber
- [ ] The Crisis by David Harris

- ☐ The Crucible by Arthur Miller
- ☐ The Curious Incident of the Dog in the Night-time by Mark Haddon
- ☐ The Da Vinci Code by Dan Brown
- ☐ The Diary of Virginia Woolf, Volume 4: 1931-1935 edited by Anne Olivier Bell
- ☐ The Diary of Virginia Woolf, Volumes 1, 3-5 edited by Anne Olivier Bell
- ☐ The Dirt: Confessions of the World's Most Notorious Rock Band by Tommy Lee, Vince Neil, Mick Mars and Nikki Sixx
- ☐ The Divine Comedy by Dante
- ☐ The Divine Secrets of the Ya-Ya Sisterhood by Rebecca Wells
- ☐ The Electric Kool-Aid Acid Test by Tom Woolf
- ☐ The Executioner's Song by Norman Mailer
- ☐ The Fountainhead by Ayn Rand
- ☐ The Gilmore Girls Companion by A. S. Berman
- ☐ The Gnostic Gospels by Elaine Pagels
- ☐ The Godfather: Book 1 by Mario Puzo
- ☐ The Graduate by Charles Webb
- ☐ The Grapes of Wrath by John Steinbeck
- ☐ The Great Gatsby by F.Scott Fitzgerald
- ☐ The Group by Mary McCarthy
- ☐ The History of the Decline and Fall of the Roman Empire by Edward Gibbon
- ☐ The History of Tom Thumb by Anonymous
- ☐ The Holy Barbarians by Lawrence Lipton
- ☐ The House of the Spirits by Isabel Allende
- ☐ The Human Factor by Graham Greene
- ☐ The Hunchback of Notre Dame by Victor Hugo
- ☐ The Iliad and The Odyssey by Homer
- ☐ The Invitation by Oriah Mountain Dreamer

- ☐ The Joy Luck Club by Amy Tan
- ☐ The Jumping Frog by Mark Twain
- ☐ The Last Empire: Essays 1992-2000 by Gore Vidal
- ☐ The Last Word by Graham Greene
- ☐ The Legend of Bagger Vance by Steven Pressfield
- ☐ The Life-Changing Magic of Tidying Up by Marie Konde'
- ☐ The Lion, The Witch, and the Wardrobe by C.S. Lewis
- ☐ The Little Locksmith by Katharine Butler Hathaway
- ☐ The Little Match Girl by Hans Christian Andersen
- ☐ The Lord of the Rings by J.R.R. Tolkien
- ☐ The Lottery by Shirley Jackson
- ☐ The Lovely Bones by Alice Sebold
- ☐ The Manticore by Robertson Davies
- ☐ The Master and the Margarita by Mikhail Bulgakov
- ☐ The Meditations by Marcus Aurelius
- ☐ The Merry Wives of Windsor by William Shakespeare
- ☐ The Metamorphosis by Franz Kafka
- ☐ The Miracle Worker by William Gibson
- ☐ The Mojo Collection: The Ultimate Music Companion by Jim Irvin
- ☐ The Mourning Bride by William Congreve
- ☐ The Naked and the Dead by Norman Mailer
- ☐ The Nancy Drew Series by Carolyn Keene
- ☐ The New Poems of Emily Dickinson by Emily Dickinson

- ☐ The New Way Things Work by David McCauley
- ☐ The Old Man and the Sea by Ernest Hemingway
- ☐ The Oresteia: Agamemnon; The Libation Bearers; The Eumenides by W.B. Stanford
- ☐ The Original Valerie's Cat Eye sCream by Valerie Campbell
- ☐ The Outbreak of the Peloponnesian War by Donald Kagan
- ☐ The Outsiders by S.E. Hinton
- ☐ The Persian Puzzle by Kenneth M Pollack
- ☐ The Picture of Dorian Gray by Oscar Wilde
- ☐ The Portable Dorothy Parker by Dorothy Parker
- ☐ The Portable Nietzche by Fredrich Nietzche
- ☐ The Price of Loyalty: George W. Bush, the White House, and the Education of Paul O'Neill by Ron Suskind
- ☐ The Princess Bride by William Golding
- ☐ The Pursuit of Love & Love in a Cold Climate by Nancy Mitford
- ☐ The Raven by Edgar Allan Poe
- ☐ The Rough Guide to Europe, 2003 Edition
- ☐ The Scarecrow of Oz by L. Frank Baum
- ☐ The Scarlet Letter by Nathaniel Hawthorne
- ☐ The Second Sex by Simone de Beauvoir
- ☐ The Shining by Stephen King
- ☐ The Sisters: The Saga of the Mitford Family by Mary S. Lovell
- ☐ The Skin of Our Teeth by Thornton Wilder
- ☐ The Sonnets by William Shakespeare
- ☐ The Sound and the Fury by William Faulkner
- ☐ The Story of My Life by Helen Keller
- ☐ The Subsect by Jess Mariano (fictional text)

- ☐ The Sun Also Rises by Ernest Hemingway
- ☐ The Town and the City by Jack Kerouac
- ☐ The Tragedy of Richard III by William Shakespeare
- ☐ The Trial by Franz Kafka
- ☐ The Unabridged Journals of Sylvia Plath 1950-1962 by Sylvia Plath
- ☐ The Unbearable Lightness of Being by Milan Kundera
- ☐ The Vanishing Newspaper by Phillip Meyers
- ☐ The Wine Bible by Karen MacNeil
- ☐ The Wizard of Oz by L. Frank Baum
- ☐ The Women of Amy Sherman-Palladino by Scott Ryan
- ☐ The Year of Magical Thinking by Joan Didion
- ☐ The Yearling by Marjorie Kinnan Rawlings
- ☐ The Comedy of Errors by William Shakespeare
- ☐ Theatre by W Somerset Maugham
- ☐ Thunder by James Grady
- ☐ Timeline by Michael Crichton
- ☐ To Have and Have Not by Ernest Hemingway
- ☐ To Kill a Mockingbird by Harper Lee
- ☐ Trainspotting by Irvine Welsh
- ☐ Trouble in Our Backyard: Central America and the United States in the Eighties by Martin Diskin
- ☐ Tuesdays with Morrie by Mitch Album
- ☐ Ulysses by James Joyce
- ☐ Uncle Tom's Cabin by Harriet Beecher Stowe
- ☐ Understanding Power by Noam Chomsky
- ☐ US Foreign Policy and the Iran Hostage Crisis by David Patrick Houghton
- ☐ Valley of the Dolls by Jacqueline Susann

- ☐ Visions of Cody by Jack Kerouac
- ☐ Waiting for Godot by Samuel Beckett
- ☐ Walden by Henry David Thoreau
- ☐ War and Peace by Leo Tolstoy
- ☐ We Owe You Nothing- Punk Planet: The Collected Interviews edited by Daniel Sinker
- ☐ Webster's Dictionary
- ☐ What Color is Your Parachute? by Richard Nelson Bolles
- ☐ What Happened to Baby Jane? by Henry Farrell
- ☐ When Everything Changed by Gail Collins
- ☐ Who Moved My Cheese? by Spencer Johnson
- ☐ Who's Afraid of Virginia Woolf? by Edward Albee
- ☐ Who's Who & What's What in Shakespeare by Evangeline M. O'Connor
- ☐ Wild by Cheryl Strayed
- ☐ Written in Blood by Dianne Fanning
- ☐ Written in Blood: the Story of the Haitian People 1492-1995 by Nancy Gordon Heinl, Robert Debs Heinl
- ☐ Wuthering Heights by Emily Bronte
- ☐ Yoga for Dummies by Georg Feuerstein and Larry Payne
- ☐ You Deserve Love by D. Sherber
- ☐ You've Been Gilmored!: The Unofficial Gilmore Girls Encyclopedia by Taryn Dryfhout
- ☐ Zorba the Greek by Nikos Kazantakis

Notes

Eternal Damnation is what I'm Risking for My Rock n Roll

Music

- ☐ (Take Me) Riding In My Car by Woody Guthrie
- ☐ 18 And Life by Skid Row
- ☐ 20th Century Girl by Pizzicato Five
- ☐ 40 Years by House of Freaks
- ☐ 52 Girls by B-52's
- ☐ 99 Luftballons by Nena
- ☐ A Beaver Ate My Thumb by Daniel Palladino
- ☐ A Cockeyed Optimist by Rogers and Hammerstein
- ☐ A Foggy Day in London Town by Frank Sinatra
- ☐ A Kiss to Build a Dream On by Louis Armstrong
- ☐ A Mighty Fortress is Our God written by Martin Luthor
- ☐ A String of Pearls by Glenn Miller
- ☐ A Whiter Shade Of Pale by Procol Harum
- ☐ ABC by Jackson 5
- ☐ Act of Love by Neil Young
- ☐ Agoraphobia by Incubus
- ☐ All Fired Up by Tralala
- ☐ All My Life by The Point
- ☐ Amazing Glow by Joe Pernice
- ☐ Amazing Grace by John Newton
- ☐ Amazing Grace in Korean
- ☐ Angels We Have Heard on High
- ☐ Angst in My Pants by Sparks
- ☐ Aquarius by The Fifth Dimension
- ☐ Archives by Louise Goffin
- ☐ Around the World by Daft Punk
- ☐ As time goes by Made famous by Sinatra
- ☐ Ave Maria by Franz Schubert
- ☐ B-A-B-Y by Rachel Sweet

- [ ] Baby Face by Bennie Davise and Harry Akst
- [ ] Baby One More Time by Britney Spears
- [ ] Bad Moon Rising by Creedence Clearwater Revival
- [ ] Ballet Waltz #3 by Herman Beeftink
- [ ] Ballo, e canto de' villanelli by Antonio Vivald
- [ ] Be True To Your School by Grant Lee Phillips
- [ ] Beanbag Chair by Yo La Tengo
- [ ] Beautiful Dreamers by Grant Lee Phillips
- [ ] Begin the Beguine by Cole Porter
- [ ] Bei Mir Bist du Schon by The Andrew Sisters
- [ ] Bette Davis Eyes by Kim Carnes
- [ ] Big Blue Buzz by Ric Menck
- [ ] Big in Japan by Tom Waits
- [ ] Blankest Year by Nada Surf
- [ ] Bluebird by The Rosebuds
- [ ] Botch-A-Me (Ba-Ba-Baciami Piccina) by Rosemary Clooney
- [ ] Boys Don't Cry by The Cure
- [ ] Bright Future In Sales by Fountains Of Wayne
- [ ] Bubbles: by The Free Design
- [ ] Buff Right
- [ ] Burning Down the House by Talking Heads
- [ ] By the Beautiful Sea performed by the Swingin Deacons
- [ ] Bye Bye Blackbird by Peggy Lee
- [ ] Calling All Enthusiasts by Radio 4
- [ ] Can't Stand Me Now by the Libertines
- [ ] Candy Man by Sammy Davis, Jr
- [ ] Car Song by Elastica
- [ ] Castle Of Spirits by Parvaneh Butterfly & Jonny Franco
- [ ] Catch a Wave by the Beach Boys

- ☐ Cat's in The Cradle by Harry Chapin
- ☐ Ce petit coeur [This Small Heart] by Francoise Hardy
- ☐ Celebration by Kool and the Gang
- ☐ Chain Gang by Sam Cooke
- ☐ Chain Gang by Sam Cooke
- ☐ Charma Chameleon by Boy George
- ☐ Cherish by The Association
- ☐ Child Psychology by Black Box Recorder
- ☐ Chimacum Rain by Linda Perhacs
- ☐ Christmas Wrapping by The Waitresses
- ☐ Church of the Poison Mind by Culture Club
- ☐ Cities in Dust by Siouxsie and the Banshees
- ☐ Come a Little Bit Closer by Jay and the Americans
- ☐ Come Fly With Me by Frank Sinatra
- ☐ Come on Feel The Noize by Slade
- ☐ Come On-A My house by Rosemary Clooney
- ☐ Conscience Clean (I Went to Spain) by Pernice Brothers
- ☐ Crazy Beat by Blur
- ☐ Crazy by Patsy Cline
- ☐ Crosseyed And Painless by Talking Heads
- ☐ Crystal Lake by Grandaddy
- ☐ Dance This Mess Around by B-52's
- ☐ Dance To The Underground by Radio 4
- ☐ Deck the Halls
- ☐ Deora AR Mo Chroi by Enya
- ☐ Diamond Dogs by David Bowie
- ☐ Do That There by Lyrics Born
- ☐ Do You Love Me from Fiddler on the Roof

- ☐ Do You Really Want to Hurt Me? by Culture Club
- ☐ Don't Know Why (You Stay) by The Essex Green
- ☐ Don't Go Sit Under The Apple Tree by The Andrew Sisters
- ☐ Don't Mug Yourself by The Streets
- ☐ I Do The Rock by Tim Curry
- ☐ Don't Sleep on the Subway by Petula Clark
- ☐ Down by Pidgeon
- ☐ Drunk by North Green
- ☐ Du Hast by Rammstein
- ☐ Dust That Dreams of Brooms by Aveo
- ☐ Early in the Morning by Buckwheat Zydeco
- ☐ Earn Enough for Us by XTC
- ☐ Easter Parade by Judy Garland
- ☐ Eleanor Put Your Boots on by Franz Ferdinand
- ☐ Endless Love by Lionel Ritchie and Diana Ross
- ☐ Eternal Flame by the Bangles
- ☐ Everlong by The Foo Fighters
- ☐ Everybody Have Fun Tonight by Wang Chung
- ☐ Everybody Needs a Little Sanctuary by Grant Lee Phillips
- ☐ Everyday I Write the Book by Elvis Costello
- ☐ Fade Into You by Mazzy Star
- ☐ Fell in Love with a Girl by The White Stripes
- ☐ Fever by Peggy Lee
- ☐ Fillmore Blues by Chuck Berry
- ☐ Fingersnap by Chucho Merchan
- ☐ Flower Girl in Bordeaux by Esquivel
- ☐ Fly Away by Lenny Kravitz
- ☐ Fly Me to the Moon by Frank Sinatra
- ☐ Folsom Prison Blues by Johnny Cash

- ☐ Freaking Out by Graham Coxon
- ☐ Ant Music by Adam and the Ants
- ☐ Friendship by Judy Garland and Johnny Mercer
- ☐ From Red to Blue by Billy Bragg
- ☐ Fuckin' Up by Neil Young
- ☐ Funky Days are Back Again by Cornershop
- ☐ Funkytown by Lipps Inc.
- ☐ Funny Face by Fred Astaire
- ☐ Genius of Love by Tom Tom Club
- ☐ Get Happy by Judy Garland
- ☐ Get The Party Started by Pink
- ☐ Get Yourself Together by Tahiti 80
- ☐ Girl From Mars by Ash
- ☐ Girls Just Wanna Have Fun by Cyndi Lauper
- ☐ God Only Knows by Claudine Longet
- ☐ Gonna Fly Now Theme from *Rocky* by Bill Conti
- ☐ Gotango by Olof Roter
- ☐ Greatest American Hero - (Believe it or Not) by Joey Scarbury
- ☐ Gypsies, Tramps, and Thieves by Cher
- ☐ Hang Down Your Head Tom Dooley by Kingston Trio
- ☐ Hanging On The Telephone by Blondie
- ☐ Happy Birthday by Mildred J. Hill and Dr. Patty Smith Hill
- ☐ Happy Days Are Here Again by Guy Lombard
- ☐ Happy Kid by Nada Surf
- ☐ Happy Song by Milkshake
- ☐ Happy X-Mas by John Lennon and Yoko Ono
- ☐ Hava Nagila a Jewish folk song
- ☐ Head On by Jesus And Mary Jane

- ☐ Heart of Glass by Blondie
- ☐ Heartland by George Strait
- ☐ Heavenly by Grant Lee Phillips
- ☐ Heavy Metal Drummer by Wilco
- ☐ Hello Dolly by Louis Armstrong
- ☐ Here They Go by Sam Phillips
- ☐ Here You Come Again by Dolly Parton
- ☐ Hero Takes a Fall by The Bangles
- ☐ Hiding in The Trees by Mindcleaner
- ☐ Holding on to the Earth by Sam Phillips
- ☐ Hollaback Girl by Gwen Stefani
- ☐ Honey Don't Think by Grant Lee Buffalo
- ☐ Hong Kong Garden by Siouxsie and the Banshees
- ☐ Hot Blooded by Foreigner
- ☐ How to Dream by Sam Phillips
- ☐ Human Behavior by Bjork
- ☐ Hurt So Good by John Mellencamp
- ☐ Hush, Little Baby (Mockingbird song)
- ☐ I Can't Get Started by Ella Fitzgerald
- ☐ I Can't Give You Anything But Love, Baby by Jimmy McHugh
- ☐ I Don't Know How to Say Goodbye to You by Sam Phillips
- ☐ I Don't Mind by Slumber Party
- ☐ I Dreamed a Dream by Anne Hathaway
- ☐ I Feel The Earth Move by Carole King
- ☐ I Found Love by the Free Design
- ☐ I Get Around by The Beach Boys
- ☐ I Think It's Gonna Rain Today by Claudine Longet
- ☐ I Thought About You by Johnny Mercer and James Van Heusen

- ☐ I Try by Macy Gray
- ☐ I Wanna Be Sedated by the Ramones
- ☐ I Will Always Love You by Dolly Parton
- ☐ I Will Always Love You by Whitney Houston
- ☐ I Won't Grow Up by Rickie Lee Jones
  Tropical Ice-Land by The Fiery Furnaces
  Pretty In Pink by The Psychedelic Furs
- ☐ I Would Go by Smoosh
- ☐ I'll Dance At Your Wedding by Vic Damone
- ☐ Ice Ice Baby by Vanilla Ice
- ☐ If I Could Write by Sam Phillips
- ☐ I'll Be Home For Christmas by Bing Crosby
- ☐ I'll Be With You In Apple Blossom Time by The Andrew Sisters
- ☐ I'll Be Your Mirror by The Velvet Underground
- ☐ I'm a Believer by The Monkees
- ☐ I'm Gonna Make You Love Me by the Jayhawks
- ☐ I'm the Man Who Murdered Love by XTC
- ☐ I'm The Man by Joe Jackson
- ☐ In a Big Country by Big Country
- ☐ In a Gadda Da Vida by Iron Butterfly
- ☐ In a Young Man's Mind by the Mooney Suzuki
- ☐ In My Honey's Lovin' Arms by Robert Mitchum
- ☐ In the Cool Cool Cool of the evening by Rosemary Clooney
- ☐ In The Mood by Glenn Miller
- ☐ Inside Out by Mighty Lemon Drops
- ☐ Iron Man by Black Sabbath
- ☐ Ironic by Alanis Morisette
- ☐ It's a Small World by Robert and Richard Sherman
- ☐ It's De-lovely by Cole Porter

- ☐ It's a Good Day by Peggy Lee
- ☐ It's Alright, Baby by Komeda
- ☐ It's Getting Hot In Herre by Nelly
- ☐ It's the Life by Grant Lee Buffalo
- ☐ Ja Glory by Toots Bombarde
- ☐ Jacqueline by Franz Ferdinand
- ☐ Jagged Little Pill by Alanis Morrissette
- ☐ Jailhouse Rock by Elvis Presley
- ☐ Jeannie Theme from I Dream of Jeannie by Buddy Kaye and Hugo Montenegro
- ☐ Johnny Angel by Shelley Fabares
- ☐ Jolene by Dolly Parton
- ☐ Jubilee by Grant Lee Buffalo
- ☐ Kiss Me by Vic Damone
- ☐ Know Your Onion by The Shins
- ☐ Kool Thing by Sonic Youth
- ☐ La Casa by Graham Preskett/Mauricio Venegas
- ☐ La La by Shark Quest
- ☐ L'anamour [The Anamour] by Jane Birkin
- ☐ Last Train to Clarksville by The Monkees
- ☐ Legal Man by Belle and Sebastian
- ☐ Let Your Ya Be Ya by Ranking Roy
- ☐ Like a Virgin by Madonna
- ☐ Lily is a Passion by Grant Lee Phillips
- ☐ Lily-A-Passion by Grant-Lee Phillips
- ☐ Lively Up Yourself by The Family Zigzag
- ☐ Livin' La Vida Loca by Ricky Martin
- ☐ Living On A Prayer by Bon Jovi
- ☐ London Calling by The Clash
- ☐ Lonesome Street by Blur
- ☐ Looks Like We Made It by Barry Manilow
- ☐ Los Angeles by X
- ☐ Lost Volvo by Mary Lynn Rajskub

- ☐ Louie Louie by Richard Berry
- ☐ Love Burns by BRMC
- ☐ L-O-V-E by Irving
- ☐ Love Is Everywhere I Go by Sam Phillips
- ☐ Love Revolution by Daniel Palladino, Jeanine Tesori
- ☐ Love Will Keep Us Together by Captain and Tennille
- ☐ Lucy in the Sky with Diamonds by William Shatner
- ☐ Lullaby by Johannes Brahm
- ☐ Maggie Blues by Bing and Gary Crosby
- ☐ Maggie's Farm by Bob Dylan
- ☐ Magic Moments by Perry Como
- ☐ Making Noises by The SqueeGees
- ☐ Mama Tried by Merle Haggard
- ☐ Mambo Italiano by Dean Martin
- ☐ Man! I Feel Like a Woman! by Shania Twain
- ☐ Man, I Feel Like a Woman! by Shania Twain
- ☐ Manic Monday by the Bangles
- ☐ Margaritaville Jimmy Buffett
- ☐ Me and Julio Down By The School Yard by Paul Simon
- ☐ Mein kleiner grüner Kaktus by the Comedian Harmonists
- ☐ Mexican Shuffle by Herb Alpert and the Tijuana Brass
- ☐ Midnight at the Oasis by Maria Muldaur
- ☐ Mixed Business by Beck
- ☐ Mockingbirds by Grant Lee Buffalo
- ☐ Mona Lisa by Grant Phillips
- ☐ Monkey Gone to Heaven by the Pixies
- ☐ Moon River by Audrey Hepburn

- ☐ Ms. Jackson by Outkast
- ☐ My Darling by Wilco
- ☐ My Favourite Letter by Stephen Lang
- ☐ My Happy Ending by Avril Lavigne
- ☐ My Heart Belongs to Daddy by Marilyn Monroe
- ☐ My Heart Belongs to Me by Barbra Streisand
- ☐ My Heart Belongs to You by Jim Brickman
- ☐ My Heart Stood Still by Ray Conniff
- ☐ My Heart Will Go On by Celine Dion
- ☐ My Little Corner of the World by Yo La Tengo
- ☐ My Melancholy Baby By Dorsey Brothers & Their Orchestra
- Man Who Sold the World by David Bowie
- ☐ My Sharona by The Knack
- ☐ Naima by John Coltrane
- ☐ Nookie by Limp Bizkit
- ☐ Nothin' is For Sure by Grant Lee Phillips
- ☐ Oblivious by Aztec Camera
- ☐ Oh My Love by John Lennon
- ☐ Oh, What A Beautiful Morning by Rodgers & Hammerstein
- ☐ On the Road Again by Willie Nelson
- ☐ One Fine Day by The Chiffons
- ☐ One For My Baby by Frank Sinatra
- ☐ One Line by PJ Harvey
- ☐ One Step Beyond by Madness
- ☐ One Way or Another by Blondie
- ☐ O'Oh by Yoko Ono
- ☐ Our Lips Are Sealed by The Go-Go's
- ☐ Peace Train by Cat Stevens
- ☐ Pennies from Heaven by Louis Armstrong
- ☐ Perfect Situation for a Fool by Jai Josefs
- ☐ Perfume by Sparks

- ☐ Piano Sonata No.2 in B Minor, Op. 35: III
- ☐ Pick Yourself Up by Fred Astaire & Ginger Rogers
- ☐ Up by Fred Astaire & Ginger Rogers
- ☐ Pictures of You by The Cure
- ☐ Pink Steam by Sonic Youth
- ☐ Pipeline by The Chantays
- ☐ Pippi Longstocking by Astrid Lindgren
- ☐ Pleasant Vally Sunday by The Monkees
- ☐ Pomp and Circumstance written by Edward Elgar
- ☐ Pre-owned heart by Grant Lee Phillips
- ☐ Price Yeah! by Pavement
- ☐ Prologue Into the Woods from the musical Into the Woods
- ☐ Purple Rain by Prince
- ☐ Raise the Spirit by Grant Lee Phillips
- ☐ Reflecting Light by Sam Phillips
- ☐ Relax by Frankie Goes To Hollywood
- ☐ Ring of Fire by Johnny Cash
- ☐ Roam by The B52s
- ☐ Robots by the Futureheads
- ☐ Rockin with the Rhythm of the Rain by The Judds
- ☐ Roxanne by The Police
- ☐ Rusholme Ruffians by The Smiths
- ☐ Russian Rhapsody by The Ossipov Balalaika orchestra, Nikolai Kalinin
- ☐ 'S Wonderful by Audrey Hepburn & Fred Astaire
- ☐ Saccharine by Sunday's Best
- ☐ Saddest Quo by Pernice Brothers
- ☐ Sadie, Sadie by Barbra Streisand

- ☐ Sadness Soot by Grant Lee Phillips
- ☐ Santa Claus is Coming to Town by Tony Bennett
- ☐ Satellite of Love by Lou Reed
- ☐ Saturday Night's Alright by Elton John
- ☐ Science vs. Romance by Rilo Kiley
- ☐ Selling Yourself Short by What Made Milwaukee Famous
- ☐ Semper Fidelis by John Phillip Sousa
- ☐ Seventh Son by Mose Allison
- ☐ Shadow Dancing by Andy Gibb
- ☐ Shy Boy by Bananarama
- ☐ Side Streets by Saint Etienne
- ☐ Sing Sing Sing (With a Swing) by James Horner Prima
- ☐ Six Months In A Leaky Boat by Split Enz
- ☐ Slow Hands by Interpol
- ☐ Slung-Lo by Erin McKeown
- ☐ Smile by Grant-Lee Phillips
- ☐ So Long, Farewell by Rodgers & Hammerstein
- ☐ So Says I by The Shins
- ☐ Some People by Bernadette Peters and William Parry
- ☐ Someone to Watch Over Me by Frank Sinatra
- ☐ Something Good from The Sound of Music
- ☐ Sometimes Always by Jesus and Mary Chain
- ☐ Songbird by Kenny G
- ☐ Space Oddity by David Bowie
- ☐ Spring Released by Grant Lee Phillips
- ☐ Stand By Your Man by Tammy Wynette
- ☐ Star Spangled Banner by Francis Scott Key, John Stafford Smith, and Springfield Digital Orchestra
- ☐ Starcrossed by Ash

- ☐ Stars and Stripes Forever by John Phillip Sousa
- ☐ Stayin' Alive by The Bee Gees
- ☐ Step Into My Office Baby by Belle and Sebastian
- ☐ String of Pearls by Glenn Miller
- ☐ Stuck In The Middle With You by Stealers Wheel
- ☐ Suburban Homeboy by Sparks
- ☐ Suffragette City by David Bowie
- ☐ Summer by Charlotte Hatherley
- ☐ Sunday Best by Grant Lee Phillips
- ☐ Superfreak by Rick James
- ☐ Suppertime by Clark Genser
- ☐ Suspended from Class by Camera Obscura
- ☐ Swan Lake -- Ballet -- Ste Op. 20a: Sea in the Moonlight by Tchaikovsky
- ☐ Symphony No. 7 in E minor (Song of the Night) by New York Philharmonic with Henry Grossman
- ☐ Symphony No.1 in D Major, Titan, Movement IV by Gustav Mahler
- ☐ Everything I've Got (Belongs to You) by Blossom Dearie
- ☐ Take My Breath Away by Berlin
- ☐ Takin' Care of Business by Bachman-Turner Overdrive
- ☐ Taking Pictures by Sam Phillips
- ☐ Tambourine Man by William Shatner
- ☐ Teach Me Tonight by Sammy Cahn and Gene De Paul
- ☐ Tears in Heaven by Eric Clapton
- ☐ Tell Her What She Wants to Know by Sam Phillips

- ☐ Tequila by Los Lodos
- ☐ Thank Heaven for Little Girls by Maurice Chevalier
- ☐ Thanks for Christmas by XTC
- ☐ The Best Is Yet To Come by Tony Bennett
- ☐ The Boat Ashore by Michael Roe
- ☐ The Candy Man by Sammy Davis, Jr
- ☐ The Coffee Song By Bob Hilliard & Richard Miles
- ☐ The Elements Song by Tom Lehrer
- ☐ The Entertainer by Billy Joel
- ☐ The Girl From Ipanema by Fantastic Strings
- ☐ The Joker by Steve Miller Band
- ☐ The Lathe of Heaven by Scott Abels, Aaron Owens, Matthew W. Parker, David Fuentes, Brian Dixon
- ☐ The Laws Have Changed by The New Pornographers
- ☐ The Little Ol' Beggar's Bush by Flogging Molly
- ☐ The Man That Got Away by Judy Garland
- ☐ The Music Goes Round And Round by Frank Froeba & His Swing Band
- ☐ Diga Diga Doo by Mills Brothers with Duke Ellington
- ☐ The Neutral by Sonic Youth
- ☐ The Perfect Crime 2 by The Decemberists
- ☐ The Rap Song by Daniel Palladino
- ☐ The Sound of Silence by Simon and Garfunkel
- ☐ The Star-Spangled Banner by Francis Scott Key
- ☐ The Way You Look Tonight by Frank Sinatra
- ☐ The Weakest Shade Of Blue by The Pernice Brothers
- ☐ The Whiffenpoof Song by the Whiffenpoofs

- ☐ Theme from Terms of Endearment by Michael Gore, Arr. Mark Northam
- ☐ Then She Appeared by XTC
- ☐ There She Goes by The La's
- ☐ These Boots Are Made For Walkin' by Nancy Sinatra
- ☐ These Foolish Things performed by the Swingin' Deacons
- ☐ Thirteen by Big Star
- ☐ This is Hell by Elvis Costello
- ☐ This Old House by Brian Setzer Orchestra
- ☐ This Town by The Go-Go's
- ☐ Those Lazy Hazy Crazy Days of Summer by Nat King Cole
- ☐ Through the Eyes of Love (Theme from Ice Castles) by Marvin Hamlisch and Carole Bayer Sager
- ☐ Time Bomb by Rancid
- ☐ Time by Tom Watts
- ☐ Tiny Cities Made of Ashes by Modest Mouse
- ☐ To Go Home by M. Ward
- ☐ Too Much Love by LCD Soundsystem
- ☐ Too Shy by Kajagoogoo
- ☐ Top Of The World by The Carpenters
- ☐ True by Spandau Ballet
- ☐ Truly Truly by Grant Lee Phillips
- ☐ Twin Cinema by the New Pornographers
- ☐ Unbreakable by Daniel and Amy Sherman-Palladino, Jeanine Tesori
- ☐ Under The Boardwalk by Bette Midler
- ☐ Until the Real Thing Comes Along by Dean Martin
- ☐ Valley Winter Song by Grant-Lee Phillips

- ☐ Video by India Arie
- ☐ Wake Me Up (Before You Go Go) by Grant Lee Phillips
- ☐ Walk Like an Egyptian by The Bangles
- ☐ Walkin' My Baby Back Home performed by the Swingin Deacons
- ☐ Walking After Midnight by Patsy Cline
- ☐ Walking On Sunshine by Katrina And The Waves
- ☐ Waterloo by ABBA
- ☐ We Are Family by Sister Sledge
- ☐ We Are the Champions by Queen
- ☐ We Wish You a Merry Christmas
- ☐ Wedding Bell Blues by The 5th Dimension
- ☐ Wedding March by Felix Mendelssohn
- ☐ Wendy by Wesley Yang and Gavin McNett
- ☐ We're All Light by XTC
- ☐ We've Got Magic To Do by Stephen Schwartz Swan Lake, Op. 20, Suite 3 - Danse des petits cygnes by Herbert von Karajan with the Berliner Philharmoniker
- ☐ Koyaanisqatsi by Philip Glass
- ☐ What A Time It Was by Daniel May
- ☐ What a Waste by Sonic Youth
- ☐ What A Wonderful World by Joey Ramone
- ☐ What Do I Do by Sam Phillips
- ☐ What More Can I Say by Kurt Cobain
- ☐ What's There Not To Love About Stars Hollow? Daniel and Amy Sherman-Palladino, Jeanine Tesori
- ☐ Whatever Will Be, Will Be (Que Sera Sera) by Doris Day
- ☐ When The Saints Go Marching In by The Dixieland All Stars

- ☐ When You Tell Me That You Love Me by Diana Ross
- ☐ Where It's At by Beck
- ☐ Where the Colors Don't Go by Sam Phillips
- ☐ Where You Lead by Carole King
- ☐ White Lines by Grandmaster and Melle Mel
- ☐ White Riot by The Clash
- ☐ Who Will Save Your Soul by Jewel
- ☐ Who's That Girl? by White and Schogger
- ☐ Why by North Green
- ☐ Why Does it Always Rain on Me? by Travis
- ☐ Wicked Witch Theme (From The Wizard of Oz)
- ☐ William Tell Overture by St. Olaf Orchestra
- ☐ Wind Beneath My Wings by Bette Midler
- ☐ Windy by The Association
- ☐ Winter Wonderland by Bing Crosby
- ☐ Winterglow by Grant-Lee Phillips
- ☐ With A Little Help From My Friends by Joe Anderson and Jim Sturgess
- ☐ Without a Net composed by Ken Hiatt
- ☐ 'Woo Hoo' by 5.6.7.8's
- ☐ Work It by Missy Elliot
- ☐ Working on Building Stars Hollow by Daniel and Amy Sherman-Palladino, Jeanine Tesori
- ☐ Yale Bulldog Chant by Cole Porter
- ☐ You and Me by Daniel May
- ☐ You Can't Hurry Love by The Concretes
- ☐ You Never Can Tell by Chuck Berry
- ☐ You're Just in Love from Call Me Madame
- ☐ You're The Top by Cole Porter
- ☐ You've Lost That Loving Feeling by The Righteous Brothers

- ☐ Zombie by The Cranberries
- ☐ Zombie Jamboree by The Kingston Trio
- ☐ Zydeco Boogaloo by Buckwheat Zydeco

Notes

It takes years of training to eat the way we do

Eating Like a Gilmore

Quintessential Gilmore Foods

- [ ] Coffee (bonus if it's in an I.V.)
- [ ] Pizza
- [ ] Mallomars
- [ ] Red Vines
- [ ] Milk Duds
- [ ] Pudding
- [ ] Cake
- [ ] Indian Food
- [ ] Chinese Food
- [ ] Tacos
- [ ] Burritos
- [ ] Mashed Banana on Toast
- [ ] Mac and Cheese
- [ ] Cherry Danish
- [ ] Fries (the devil's starchy fingers)
- [ ] Burgers
- [ ] Ice cream
- [ ] Donuts
- [ ] Pop Tarts
- [ ] Hamburger Helper
- [ ] Pie
- [ ] Pancakes
- [ ] Santa burger
- [ ] Zima
- [ ] Desert Sushi

Notes

In Omnia Paratus

The Gilmore Girls Bucket List

- ☐ Go on a hayride (1.1)
- ☐ Name your child after yourself (1.1)
- ☐ Play volleyball (1.1)
- ☐ Take a business class at college (1.1)
- ☐ Join the German Club (1.2)
- ☐ Play golf at the Country Club (1.3)
- ☐ Take a steam (1.3)
- ☐ Date a teacher (1.5)
- ☐ Get your face printed on a birthday cake (1.6)
- ☐ Kiss the boy in the grocery store and shoplift cornstarch (1.7)
- ☐ Watch Willy Wonka and the Chocolate Factory and eat junk food (1.7)
- ☐ Take a walk in the first snow of the season (1.8)
- ☐ Go to a black and white movie on a first date (1.8)
- ☐ Go to a dance with your gentleman caller (1.9)
- ☐ Kiss said gentleman caller on the dance floor (1.9)
- ☐ Exchange a gift for a semi-pornographic leering monkey lamp (1.9)
- ☐ Take part in the community Christmas production (1.10)
- ☐ Go on a double date (1.12)
- ☐ Go to a Bangles concert (1.13)
- ☐ Buy some clothes from a rummage sale (1.13)
- ☐ Watch the Donna Reed Show and eat pizza (1.14)
- ☐ Hold a Donna Reed night (1.14)
- ☐ Go watch a community softball game (1.15)
- ☐ Re-arrange your lounge furniture (1.17)
- ☐ Wallow (1.17)

- ☐ Make a list of all the things you intend on doing on weekends, but never get around to. Then fulfill the list (1.17)
- ☐ Go to a party, stay till at least 10.30pm and catch up on your reading (1.17)
- ☐ Explore an old abandoned Inn (1.19)
- ☐ See an old movie at the local cinema (1.19)
- ☐ Play 1, 2, 3, He's Yours! (1.20)
- ☐ Volunteer at a charity building project (2.2)
- ☐ Have a wedding shower (2.2)
- ☐ Sample wedding cakes (2.3)
- ☐ Have a bachelorette party (2.3)
- ☐ Go on an impromptu road trip (2.3)
- ☐ Stop at a roadside nut stall (2.4)
- ☐ Stay at a B&B and sign the guestbook (2.4)
- ☐ Visit Harvard University and buy merchandise (2.4)
- ☐ Use 'existentialist' in a sentence (2.4)
- ☐ 'Come out' at a debutante ball (2.6)
- ☐ Learn the Viennese Waltz (2.8)
- ☐ Join a secret society (2.7)
- ☐ Join the booster club (2.7)
- ☐ Take part in a fashion show (2.7)
- ☐ Act in a Shakespeare play (2.9)
- ☐ Hold an authentic 'Bracebridge' dinner (2.10)
- ☐ Enter a snowman competition (2.10)
- ☐ Dress up and go see the Rocky Horror Picture Show (2.11)
- ☐ Get photo printed pyjamas (2.11)
- ☐ Join the cheerleading team (2.11)
- ☐ Plan the family burial spaces (2.12)
- ☐ Go on a romantic picnic date (2.13)
- ☐ Get pizza and hit the bookstore (2.13)

- ☐ Jump into a pile of dirty laundry (2.14)
- ☐ Play bagel hockey (2.14)
- ☐ Take part in a formal debate (2.14)
- ☐ Hire a local teenager to clean your rain gutters (2.14)
- ☐ Buy a clock radio that makes barnyard animal noises (2.15)
- ☐ Go on a spa weekend with your mother (2.16)
- ☐ Go to a 60/40 bar for a steak (2.16)
- ☐ Graduate from community college (2.21)
- ☐ Shoot clay pigeons (2.21)
- ☐ Have an after finals margherita (2.21)
- ☐ Buy a hot dog from a street cart (2.21)
- ☐ Go on the subway (2.21)
- ☐ Be in your best friend's wedding (2.22)
- ☐ Go to Martha's Vineyard for the summer (3.1)
- ☐ Visit the Smithsonian Museum (3.1)
- ☐ Dye your hair bright purple (3.3)
- ☐ Attend a vintage auction (3.5)
- ☐ Attend a baby shower (3.6)
- ☐ Participate in a dance-a-thon (3.7)
- ☐ Take a class at the local learning center (3.11)
- ☐ Take a fencing class (3.11)
- ☐ Attend a family wedding of your best friend (3.12)
- ☐ Clean out your garage (3.12)
- ☐ Go on a fishing date (3.12)
- ☐ Be accepted into Ivy League colleges (3.16)
- ☐ Have a birthday party with the world's biggest pizza (almost) (3.18)
- ☐ Wind up as the grad night treasurer for the Booster club (3.19)

- ☐ Go backpacking around Europe before college (3.22)
- ☐ Try out all the takeaway outlets in your area and rate them according to a system (4.1)
- ☐ Plant bulbs from your neighbor because cultivating new life which will help distract from your current emptiness and sense of loss (4.5)
- ☐ Go to a food court for a smorgasbord lunch (4.15)
- ☐ Go window shopping, walking arm in arm like movie ladies (4.15)
- ☐ Have a pizza and The Power of Myth night (4.17)
- ☐ Attend a live public book reading (4.19)
- ☐ Open an Inn (4.22)
- ☐ Join a Barbershop Quartet (5.5)
- ☐ Do a 'bumper sticker test' (5.7)
- ☐ Don't use the letter "E" for an entire evening (5.7)
- ☐ Go glamping with a safari theme (5.7)
- ☐ Have an ice rink built in your front yard (5.11)
- ☐ Renew your wedding vows (5.13)
- ☐ Have your business feature in a magazine (5.18)
- ☐ Take a newspaper internship (5.19)
- ☐ Sponsor a dancer (5.21)
- ☐ Throw your best friend a baby shower (5.21, 7.16)
- ☐ Steal a yacht (5.21)
- ☐ Drop out of college (5.22)
- ☐ Move in with your grandparents (5.22)
- ☐ Get engaged (6.1)
- ☐ Join the DAR (6.3)
- ☐ Go on a tour with your band (6.3)

- ☐ Be a godmother to your best friend's baby (6.4)
- ☐ Run a 1940s, Hollywood canteen themed fundraiser (6.4)
- ☐ Have a 21st birthday party (6.7)
- ☐ Get a part-time job writing for a newspaper (6.9)
- ☐ Go back to college after a semester long break (6.10)
- ☐ Go to Atlantic city for your 21st birthday, play 21, buy 21 things and get 21 guys' phone numbers (6.11)
- ☐ Be evaluated by a psychologist (6.11)
- ☐ Become the editor of your college newspaper (6.14)
- ☐ Give your father a tour of your college campus (6.14)
- ☐ Go on a Valentine's weekend getaway to Martha's Vineyard (6.15)
- ☐ Go to the gym to drink cucumber water and get a massage (6.15)
- ☐ Ruin your friend's wedding dress (6.18)
- ☐ Have a college building named after you (6.22)
- ☐ Throw a bon voyage party (6.22)
- ☐ Take a job teaching SAT Prep (7.3)
- ☐ Attend an art show (7.4)
- ☐ Go on a private drive-in movie date (7.4)
- ☐ Pick your mother up from jail (7.4)
- ☐ Go to Paris and elope (7.7)
- ☐ Plan a wedding party (7.10)
- ☐ Go out with friends to an Indian restaurant (7.10)
- ☐ Go spend Christmas overseas with a boyfriend (7.11)

- ☐ Make cookies from scratching (7.11)
- ☐ Make popcorn and cranberry strings (7.11)
- ☐ Go out for candy cane coffee (7.11)
- ☐ Write a character reference for a friend (7.11)
- ☐ Babysit so a friend can go skiing (7.12)
- ☐ Have a flat-screen T.V. installed at home (7.12)
- ☐ Write an apology to a friend (7.12)
- ☐ Go tray sliding (7.12)
- ☐ Attend a dog funeral (7.14)
- ☐ Go through a haybale maze (7.18)
- ☐ Get your ears pierced like (7.18)
- ☐ Attend a Spring Fling festival (7.18)
- ☐ Bring your boyfriend home for the weekend (7.18)
- ☐ Read the newspaper while you take a train ride (7.18)
- ☐ Write a pro/con list (7.18)
- ☐ Get a job writing for a local newspaper (7.18)
- ☐ Be accepted into Yale Law school (7.19)
- ☐ Be accepted into Harvard Medical School (7.19)
- ☐ Be accepted into the University of Pennsylvania School of Medicine (7.19)
- ☐ Be accepted into Columbia University (7.19)
- ☐ Be accepted into Stanford University (7.19)
- ☐ Ride your bike to work (7.19)
- ☐ Plan a six-week cruise down the coast of Maine (7.20)
- ☐ Visit the Mark Twain Museum (7.20)
- ☐ Go to a karaoke night (7.20)
- ☐ Spackle the walls (7.21)
- ☐ Visit a piece of street performance art (7.21)
- ☐ Have a graduation party (7.21)
- ☐ Graduate from Yale University (7.21)

- ☐ Meet Christiane Amanpour (7.22)
- ☐ Plan a roller coaster trip around the U.S. (7.22)
- ☐ Get a job writing for an online magazine (7.22)
- ☐ Throw a surprise party (7.22)
- ☐ Learn tap dancing for relaxation (AYITL: Winter)
- ☐ Move back home (AYITL: Winter)
- ☐ Start things up with an old lover (AYITL: Winter)
- ☐ Use a local ride share company (AYITL: Winter)
- ☐ Clear your house according to Marie Kondo's method (AYITL: Winter)
- ☐ Go to therapy with a family member (AYITL: Spring)
- ☐ Go to an international food festival (AYITL: Spring)
- ☐ Go to the pool (AYITL: Summer)
- ☐ Go to a tango club (AYITL: Fall)
- ☐ Organise a flash mob for your wedding (AYITL: Fall)
- ☐ Get married (AYITL: Fall)
- ☐ Drink wine in a gazebo (AYITL: Fall)
- ☐ Get pregnant (AYITL: Fall)

Other:

- ☐ Read all of the books in this book
- ☐ Watch all of the movies in this book
- ☐ Watch all of the television shows in this book
- ☐ Make all of the food in the 'Eat like a Gilmore' Cookbooks
- ☐ Attend a town meeting
- ☐ Live in a small town, and take part in community events
- ☐ Go to the annual fan festival
- ☐ Listen to the Gilmore Guys podcasts

Notes

What She Tackles, She Conquers

How to Study Like a Gilmore

High School

- ☐ Utilize class time to work on assignments (1.1)
- ☐ Take a business class at your local community college (1.1)
- ☐ Maintain a 4.0 (1.2)
- ☐ Study alone, and decline invitations to study with others (1.2)
- ☐ Turn down ice cream during study sessions (1.4)
- ☐ Pull an all-nighter when you are cramming for a test (1.4)
- ☐ Have your mum speak with the headmaster when you miss your test (1.4)
- ☐ Attend class, even on your birthday (1.6)
- ☐ Attend the college fair every year (1.6)
- ☐ Take notes during class (1.13)
- ☐ Host group projects at your house (1.13)
- ☐ Take time off from studying to help out a friend (1.18)
- ☐ Fall asleep with your study materials (1.19)
- ☐ Listen to gloomy music during study sessions (1.19)
- ☐ Enrol in summer school (2.2)
- ☐ Do volunteer work to boost your college applications (2.2)
- ☐ Take a night to plan your extracurriculars (2.2)
- ☐ Join the high school newspaper (2.5)
- ☐ Catch up on your reading while you are waiting for meetings to start (2.5)
- ☐ Buy folders to keep your notes neat (2.5)
- ☐ Get good scores on the PSAT's (2.11)

- ☐ Attend school every single day (2.12)
- ☐ Have study session/sleepovers (2.16)
- ☐ Run for student body president (2.22)
- ☐ Spend a summer as an intern in Washington (3.1)
- ☐ Make sure nobody knows that you were watching the Brady bunch Variety Hour when your college applications arrive (3.3)
- ☐ Learn to go from 'zero to studying' in less than 60 seconds (3.6)
- ☐ Take an alumni tour of a university campus (3.8)
- ☐ Apply to other colleges as 'back-ups' (3.9)
- ☐ Apply for the school speech competition (3.16)
- ☐ Stay a virgin so that you will get into Harvard (3.16)
- ☐ Make a pro/con list to decide which college you will attend (3.17)
- ☐ Attend school even once you have matriculated (3.17)
- ☐ Request extra graduation tickets (3.19)
- ☐ Make a list of "things to do before graduation" (3.21)
- ☐ Switch subjects back and forth when studying for finals to maximize productivity (3.21)
- ☐ Stay up and study even when you are excited (3;.21)
- ☐ Graduate high school (3.22)
- ☐ Borrow your college tuition from your grandparents (3.22)
- ☐ Give the valedictorian speech at your graduation (3.22)
- ☐ Have an after-grad party at your house (3.22)

College

Freshman

- ☐ Attend college orientation and memorize the schedule (4.1)
- ☐ Take your own mattress to your dorm room (4.1)
- ☐ Make notes at orientation (4.1)
- ☐ Have your Mom come and stay the night on your first night at college (4.1)
- ☐ Hold a take-out party in your dorm room to try all the takeaways in the area (4.1)
- ☐ Howl back to the guys in the dorm (4.1)
- ☐ Go to "shopping week" - pick 50 classses, plus another 10 to squeeze in if you have time (4.3)
- ☐ Rush to your first class like an hour early (4.3)
- ☐ Leave your door open for the dorm floor party to get to know the other students (4.3)
- ☐ Take a course in 'Japanese fiction' (4.3)
- ☐ Get a haircut to celebrate your newfound independence (4.4)
- ☐ Go home in the weekend for the perfect Stars Hollow day - hang out in town, read, veg, drink coffee and hit Luke's for a late lunch (4.4)
- ☐ Take your reading, homework, and laundry home for the weekend (4.5)
- ☐ Take five courses at a time, because you like to be busy (4.6)
- ☐ Find a quiet place to study, even if it means paying someone $20 to sit under your study tree (4.6)
- ☐ Write articles for the college newspaper (4.8)

- ☐ Write theatre reviews that eviscerate people (4.8)
- ☐ Use the internet for research (4.8)
- ☐ Go into finals induced hibernation (4.9)
- ☐ Take a course in 'Contemporary Political Fiction' (4.10)
- ☐ Contribute to group discussions in class (4.11)
- ☐ Join the International Relations Club (4.12)
- ☐ Take game theory (4.14)
- ☐ Pad a paper from one course with research from another (4.14)
- ☐ Drop a course after receiving a D paper (4.14)
- ☐ Nap between classes (4.14)
- ☐ Take Major English Poets (4.14)
- ☐ Borrow notes from a classmate so you can skip a class (4.14)
- ☐ Play hooky to go window shipping (4.15)
- ☐ Pick up a part-time job as a food hall card swiper (4.14)
- ☐ Use the newsroom resources to research a family obituary (4.16)
- ☐ Sign up to man a petition table (4.17)
- ☐ Go on Spring Break in Florida (4.17)
- ☐ Go home during weekends to concentrate on upcoming assignments (4.18)
- ☐ Question your grade with your professor (4.19)
- ☐ Take 'Philosophy' (4.21)
- ☐ Think about Kafka and Chaucer even when your finals are finished (4.21)
- ☐ Get a summer job so that you can save and avoid a semester time job (4.22)

Sophomore

- ☐ Move into Branford College (5.3)
- ☐ Secure the position of Feature Writer at the college newspaper (5.6)
- ☐ Stay in the newspaper office late to work on a scoop (5.6)
- ☐ Take 'Comparative Religions' (5.8)
- ☐ Attend a Yale alumni party (5.8)
- ☐ Study with a friend (5.9)
- ☐ Host a student from your old high school, and show them college life (5.10)
- ☐ Take 'Morals and Principles' (5.11)
- ☐ Take 'Modern Poetry' (5.12)
- ☐ Accept an internship at a local newspaper (5.19)
- ☐ Sit through your final in a haze, and do not complete it (5.22)
- ☐ Drop out of Yale, after deflating comments from a mentor upset you (5.22)
- ☐ Take 'Poetry' (7.12)

Junior

- ☐ Go back to Yale (6.9)
- ☐ Be pushy until you are offered a writing position at a newspaper (6.9)
- ☐ Add to courses to your study load so that you graduate at the time that you would have (6.11)
- ☐ Make notes while you walk (6.13)

☐ Buy and wear college merchandise (6.14)
☐ Become the editor of your college newspaper (6.14)
☐ Take 'Micro Economics' (6.14)
☐ Take part in a journalism panel (6.16)

Senior

☐ Take a job teaching SAT Prep (7.3)
☐ Review an art exhibition for the college newspaper (7.4)
☐ Take "Economics" (7.5)
☐ Major in English (7.5)
☐ Host your parents at "Parents Weekend" (7.6)
☐ Get to class on time (7.6)
☐ Take 'Major English Poets' (7.8)
☐ Network at parties (7.8)
☐ Submit articles for an online magazine (7.8)
☐ Submit a piece for an online publication (7.8)
☐ Draw up on 'Operation Finish line" (7.12)
☐ Use your academic connections to get letters of recommendation (7.12)
☐ Boost your resume with volunteer work (7.12)
☐ Work on your resume (7.14)
☐ Meet with a top journalist to make connections (7.16)
☐ Apply for the Reston fellowship (7.16)
☐ Set up interviews at newspapers (7.17)
☐ Take '20th Century Poets' (7.19)

Post-College

- ☐ Write an article about people waiting in lines (AYITL: Spring)
- ☐ Look for your lucky outfit (AYITL: Spring)
- ☐ Go to Alumni Day and speak at your old high school (AYITL: Spring)
- ☐ Take an interview with an online publication which headhunted you (AYITL: Spring)
- ☐ Take a job as editor of a local newspaper (AYITL: Summer)
- ☐ Outline an autobiographical book (AYITL: Summer)
- ☐ Stay in a house by yourself to work on your book (AYITL: Fall)

Notes

_____
_____
_____
_____
_____
_____
_____

About the Author

Taryn is an experienced writer, English teacher, theologian, and coffee junkie who lives in New Zealand with her husband and four children.

A Rory-inspired blue-stocking, Taryn is a serial student, earning several diploma's and degrees, and now currently completing a PhD program. She works part-time as a college tutor, and has won awards for her post-graduate research and Māori leadership.

Taryn's publication record includes several non-fiction books, tertiary college courses, website content, and more than 400 feature articles, reviews, and columns published in newspapers, websites, and magazines.

When Taryn is not writing, studying, or with her kids, she can be found reading books, buying books, or watching *Gilmore Girls*.

www.TarynDryfhout.com

www.ingramcontent.com/pod-product-compliance
Lightning Source LLC
Chambersburg PA
CBHW051454290426
44109CB00016B/1755